*After You've Said,
"I Believe"*

After you've said, "I believe"

by LeRoy "Pat" Patterson
Chaplain, Wheaton College

Tyndale House
Publishers, Inc.
Wheaton, Illinois

Library of Congress
Catalog Card Number
78-57965.
ISBN 0-8423-0056-2,
paper.
Copyright © 1979
H. LeRoy Patterson,
All rights reserved.
First printing, April
1979.
Printed in the United
States of America.

*Dedicated
to all young believers
who have had difficulty
in getting it all
together.*

CONTENTS

Preface 9

Introduction: What's Gotten into You? 11

1 You've Got to Be Kidding, Lord! / The New Birth 15

2 Sprouting Wings or Growing Horns? / The Two Natures 21

3 Godly Amnesia / Forgiveness 25

4 Disciple or Follower? / Commitment 31

5 Getting to Know You / Prayer 35

6 Getting Zonked with Begats / The Bible 43

7 Is There Anybody Out There? / God the Father 53

8 A Crisis of Identity / God the Son 59

9 Holy What? / God the Holy Spirit 69

10 Dart Board Diplomacy / Guidance 81

11 Who Needs the Church? / Ministry 89

12 This Little Light of Mine / Witness 95

13 Where Do We Go from Here? / Last Things 101

14 Keeping the Battery Charged / Personal Devotional Life 109

Appendix: Recommended Books 117

DISCIPLE-
SHIP
A—E

PREFACE

This little booklet evolved as the result of a challenge. While in the college bookstore one day, I noticed a rather frustrated girl standing in front of a rack of books marked Discipleship. She had been leafing through one book after another, until she looked up and saw me standing there.

"I'm looking for a booklet to send to one of my friends who has recently become a Christian," she said.

"What's the matter with these?" I asked, pointing to the stack of books she had been examining.

"Oh, they are all fine," she said, "but they are either too expensive, too long, too idealistic, or too academic."

Then, brightening, she said, "Hey, why don't you write a booklet for me?" I was too flattered to refuse.

So, in response to her challenge, I have tried

to put together a booklet that, I hope, meets all of her objections. It is not expensive, not long, not idealistic, and surely not academic.

In creating this booklet I have tried to recall some of my own early frustrations and questions about the Christian life. And I have tried to resolve some of the erroneous concepts that I had been given as a young Christian.

So in a very real sense this booklet is the story of my own search for a practical experience of discipleship.

*LeRoy "Pat" Patterson, Campus Minister
Wheaton College, Wheaton, Illinois*

INTRODUCTION:
What's Gotten into You?

So you have decided to follow Jesus. That's commendable. It is the greatest decision you will ever make in your life.

Now you are probably saying to yourself, "Why did I wait so long?" Well, like some of us, you were probably waiting for God to do something really spectacular. Like hitting you over the head with a bolt of lightning. Or writing your name in letters of fire upon the wall. At the very least he could have struck you down into the dust like he did to Paul on the road to Damascus. That would surely have been impressive.

But it didn't happen like that at all, did it? Probably like many of us, you simply and quietly bowed your head and invited Jesus to come into your life and take over. You didn't have any high voltage emotional reaction, or hear any clanging of bells, or even a fanfare of trumpets. But like the soft blowing of the wind, the Holy Spirit

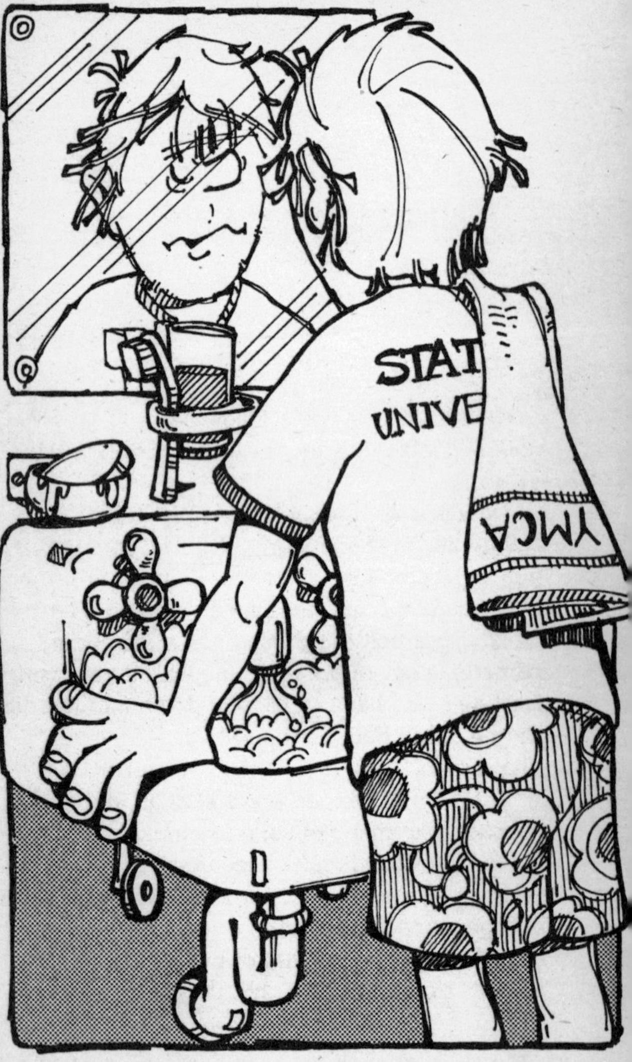
STAT
UNIVE
YMCA

breathed upon you, and you became a *"new creation in Christ"* (2 Cor. 5:17).

Like some of us, you probably got up the next morning and said to yourself, "So what else is new?" You still looked the same in the mirror. And many of the same old problems were still there, and even the same temptations. In fact, perhaps it was only your imagination, but it seemed as though the temptations were even greater than before.

But in spite of appearances, something *has* happened to you. Possibly some of your friends have asked, "What's gotten into you?" The answer is quite simple. The gracious Holy Spirit has gotten into you, and he is quietly at work there in the temple of your life.

You are probably not even aware of all that is going on within you, because it isn't happening overnight. As a matter of fact, it is a process that will continue all your life and will not be fully perfected until you enter finally into his presence. (Theologians call this process *sanctification*.)

This work of the Holy Spirit in you has some tremendous theological implications, which we will be talking about later. But in the meantime, it will be helpful to you to take the time right now to memorize and study the following supporting Scriptures.

1 Cor. 3:16 *"Don't you know that you yourselves are God's temple and that God's Spirit lives in you?"*
1 Cor. 6:19 *"Do you not know that your body is a temple of the Holy Spirit, who is in you,*

whom you have received from God?"
Phil. 2:13 *"It is God who works in you to will and to act according to his good purpose."*
Gal. 2:20 *"It is no longer I who live, but Christ who lives in me."*

ONE
You've Got to Be Kidding, Lord!

The professor of theology stood there looking at Jesus incredulously. Jesus had just told him that he needed to be "born again." He gulped once or twice, then said, "You're putting me on! How can a man be born when he is old? Can he enter the second time into his mother's womb and then be born again?"

Well, obviously Jesus wasn't kidding. Not that he was above enjoying a good practical joke, but he was in dead earnest. (Read John 3:1-9.)

The very thing that the theology prof stumbled over is the thing that has happened to you. Because you have put your trust in Jesus as your Lord you have been *born again*. The other apostles called it "regeneration," but it means the same thing.

It would be well for you at this stage to consider this aspect of your new relationship to God. You have been born into his family. This gives

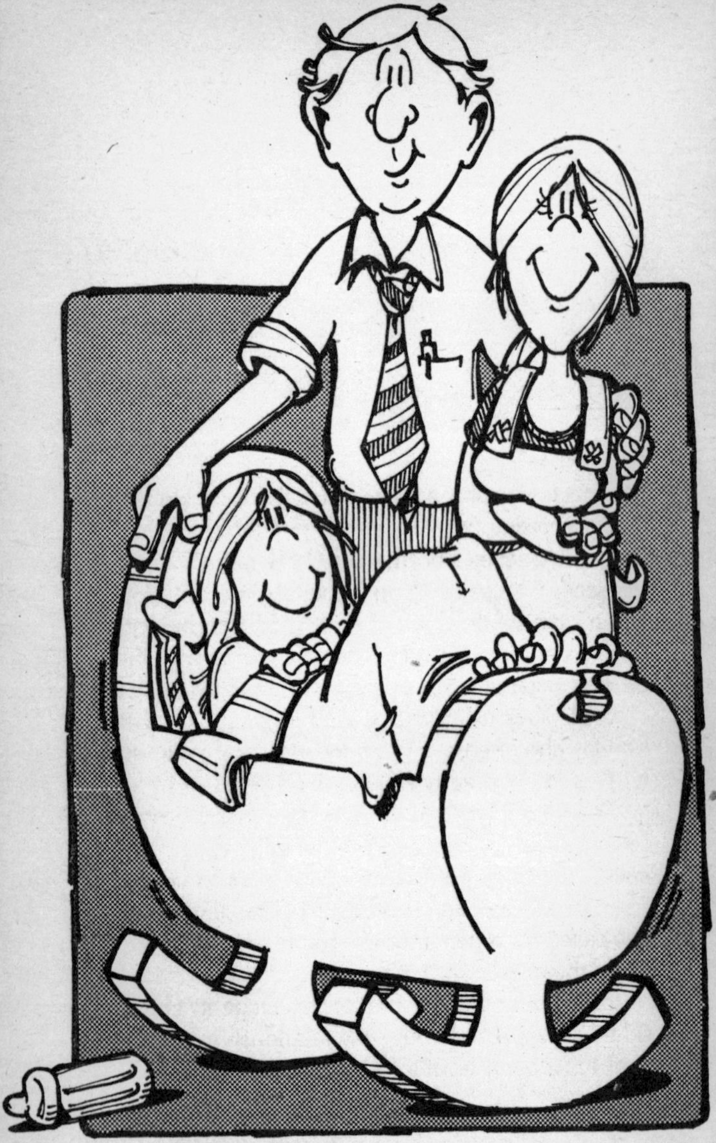

you the right to call yourself a "child of God." Other believers are your brothers and sisters, for you all have the same Father. John affirmed this in his Gospel when he wrote, *"to all who received him, who believed in his name, he gave the right to become children of God"* (John 1:12).

So, my young Christian, you now belong to the family of God. Think of that! The God of the universe is is your own personal heavenly Father.

But how did this come about? Maybe you are as puzzled as Nicodemus was when Jesus talked to him about this new birth. So, let's take a brief look at Jesus' explanation in John 3.

First, Jesus indicated that this new life is of supernatural origin. The expression *born again* in verses 3 and 7 literally means *"to be born from above."* That is, this new life comes from God; it isn't something we can generate by our own efforts. Just as we had nothing to do with the conception and birth of our physical body, neither can we produce this new life. It is *"from above."*

Second, Jesus indicated that this new life is dependent upon life-giving water. Notice the fifth verse, *"unless a man is born of water . . . he cannot see the kingdom of God."*

This verse has been interpreted various ways. It seems to me that he is talking here about the *"water"* of the Word of God. James writes, *"he chose to give us birth through the word of truth"* (James 1:18). And Peter adds, *"you have been born again, not of perishable seed, but of imperishable, through the living and enduring word of God"* (1 Pet. 1:23).

So, it was because you heard the message of

17

God's Word that the seed was implanted in your heart that was to result in the birth of your new life in Christ.

Then Jesus mentions one other important factor in this new birth experience. In that same fifth verse of John 3 Jesus said that we must be *"born of water and the Spirit,"* if we are to become members of God's family. In other words, there must also be the active involvement of the Holy Spirit in this life-giving process. Just as a human birth requires the seed of the man and the egg of the woman, so this new birth requires the seed of the Word and the life of the Spirit. And when these two life-giving agents meet together in the womb of our hearts, a new life is conceived and we are *born again*.

No, he wasn't kidding when he talked about this new birth. Let me suggest that you do two things immediately: first, pause right now and thank God for allowing you to become his child with all the privileges of being a member of God's family; second, begin now to memorize and study the verses listed here.

> John 1:12 *"To all who received him, to those who believed in his name, he gave the right to become children of God."*
> John 3:5–7 *"I tell you the truth, unless a man is born of water and of the Spirit, he cannot enter the kingdom of God. Flesh gives birth to flesh, but the Spirit gives birth to spirit. You should not be surprised at my saying, You must be born again."*

James 1:18 *"He chose to give us birth through the word of truth."*
1 Pet. 1:23 *"For you have been born again, not of perishable seed, but of imperishable, through the living and enduring word of God."*
1 John 3:1-3 *"How great is the love the Father has lavished on us, that we should be called children of God. And that is what we are! The reason the world does not know us is that it did not know him. Dear friends, now we are the children of God, and what we will be has not yet been made known. But we know that when he appears, we shall be like him, for we shall see him as he is."*

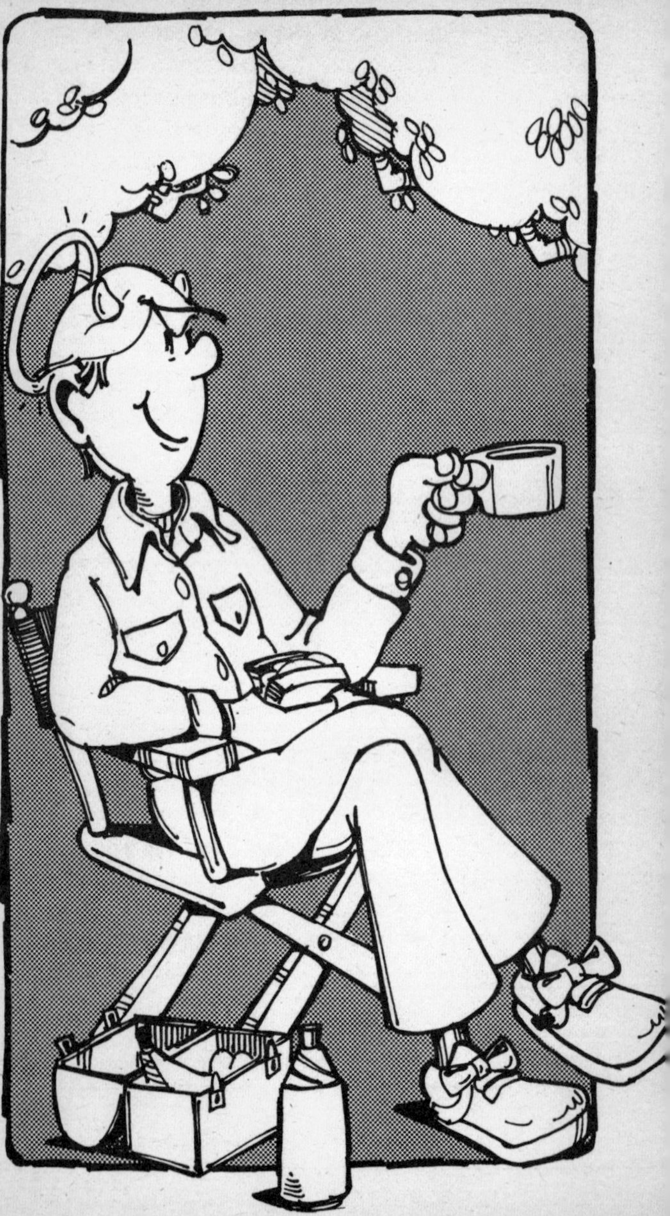

TWO
Sprouting Wings or Growing Horns?

Now that you have opened your life to the Lord everything is coming up roses. All your problems have been resolved, and you have had no more temptations. Right?

Wrong! Unless you are different from the rest of God's children, you are finding out that becoming a Christian doesn't exempt you from all of life's problems. You have already discovered that, like our confused friend in the cartoon, you aren't sure whether to sprout wings or grow horns. There are times when you feel very angelic and spiritual, but at other times you feel downright mean and hateful.

What has happened? Aren't Christians supposed to be always on top of everything? Don't they go around with stars in their eyes and idyllic smiles on their faces? Yes, sometimes. But not always.

It is well to learn at the beginning that when

we come to Christ we still have the same emotions and temperaments that we had before. We will be happy at times and sad at others. We will experience our anxious moments and our times of doubting. There will be times of great spiritual exaltation and times of utter frustration.

When these difficult times come there is always a tendency to reproach ourselves and feel very guilty. In fact, there will be a lot of well-meaning Christians who will be quick to condemn you for these feelings of inadequacy. And their condemnation will only drive you deeper into despair.

What is the problem? Well, it is simply the old story of two opposite personalities trying to live under the same roof. The moment the Holy Spirit sets up housekeeping in your life, a conflict occurs with the old tenant, called the "old man," or the "old nature." Sometimes the Bible refers to it as the "carnal nature." They are the original odd couple.

Paul explains this in Galatians 5:17, *"For the sinful nature desires what is contrary to the Spirit, and the Spirit what is contrary to the sinful nature. They are in conflict with each other, so that you do not do what you want."*

Paul himself experienced this same warfare with his old nature. (Read Romans 7:14–25.) So even such a spiritual giant as the Apostle Paul had his wrestlings with the old nature.

So, there is a war going on within you. The old nature is pulling one way, and the new nature is pulling in another. Now, it would be nice if God would simply eradicate the old nature so that we could live at peace. But that's not the way God does things.

We don't grow strong by eliminating resistance. When we do calisthenics we create resistance to build muscles and endurance. In the same way the problems of life present us with the opportunity to exercise our faith. What happens when we fail to get our physical exercise? We get fat and lazy. What is true of our bodies is also true of our spirits.

Paul illustrated this by a number of athletic analogies. He spoke of the Christian life as wrestling, running, and fighting. Anyone who has been involved in these sports knows that they are hard and demanding.

So, the conflicts of life are designed by a loving God to discipline us and to make us strong. And at the same time he has given us the necessary equipment to help us in the battle. More about those resources later.

In the meantime, take the opportunity to study and memorize the following Scriptures.

> John 16:33 *"I have told you these things, so that in me you might have peace. In the world you will have trouble. But take heart! I have overcome the world."*
> Rom. 8:35–37 *"Who shall separate us from the love of Christ? Shall trouble or hardship or persecution or famine or nakedness or danger or sword? As it is written, For your sake we face death all the day long, we are considered as sheep to be slaughtered. No, in all these*

things we are more than conquerors through him who loved us."

Rom. 13:14 *"Clothe yourselves with the Lord Jesus Christ, and do not think about how to gratify the desires of your sinful nature."*

Gal. 5:16-17 *"So I say, live by the Spirit, and you will not gratify the desires of your sinful nature. For the sinful nature desires what is contrary to the Spirit, and the Spirit what is contrary to the sinful nature. They are in conflict with each other, so that you do not do what you want."*

Rom. 7:21-25 *"When I want to do good, evil is right there with me. For in my inner being I delight in God's law; but I see another law at work in the members of my body, waging war against the law of my mind and making me prisoner to the law of sin at work within my members. What a wretched man I am! Who will rescue me from this body of death? Thanks be to God, through Jesus Christ our Lord."*

THREE
Godly Amnesia

The previous subject indicated clearly that we are in a battle. The old nature is opposed to the presence of the new nature, and keeps pulling us in the wrong direction. Even the great apostle admitted in Romans 7 that he hadn't won all the bouts with the old man. And he freely admitted that *"it is the sin that dwells within me."*

So, we are faced with this paradox. We have the potential to live a life of holiness, yet we continue to sin. Perhaps our sins are not the kind that make the headlines, but they are still very upsetting. Sometimes the sins of pride, resentment, self-seeking, and such like are not as apparent to others as the sins of drunkenness, adultery, or stealing. Nevertheless, they can be extremely damaging to us in our effort to live the Christian life.

What can we do about our sins? Well, we could rationalize them, as many people do. Or,

DAILY STAR
SALLY
CHRISTIAN
SINS AGAIN
DETAILS ON
PAGE EIGHT

we might excuse them on the ground of ignorance. Or, like some Christians, we might even pretend that they don't exist. But John knocked that one all apart when he said, *"If we claim to be without sin, we deceive ourselves and the truth is not in us"* (1 John 1:8).

John tells us in the following verse (1 John 1:9) that there is a better way to handle our sins than rationalizing them, excusing them, or ignoring them. He suggests that we confess that we have them, and claim the forgiveness of God for them. By so doing, we have the assurance that God will not only forgive us, but will keep on purifying us.

It is hard to believe that simply on the basis of our personal faith in Jesus Christ, God has forgiven us *all* our sins. But that's what makes the Christian message the Good News.

Because this sounds too simplistic, the world has totally rejected it. And even many who have professed to believe it have only given mental assent to it. They still want to earn continued forgiveness on the basis of performance. But forgiveness is purely by the grace of God. It has nothing to do with how good or bad we are, or how nobly we perform as Christians. *"For it is by grace you have been saved, through faith. And this not from yourselves, it is the gift of God, not by works, so that no one can boast"* (Eph. 2:8-9).

It is often difficult for new Christians to sense the full significance of total forgiveness. Consequently, they continue to feel guilty about sins, real or otherwise.

I have liberating news for you. In Christ, *all* your sins have been forgiven. They have been forgotten by God, and he promised never to bring them to mind. In fact, he said he would put them behind his back, and never see them again.

Now, if our righteous God has forgotten our sins, then we ought to indulge in a little godly amnesia ourselves. Why should we go about carrying a weight of guilt that God has already laid upon his Son? When Jesus died on the cross, he took upon himself the sin and guilt of all who would trust him. (Be sure to read and memorize the Scriptures listed at the conclusion of this chapter.)

When we say that Christ's death atoned for *all* our sins, we mean exactly that—not merely the sins of our past lives, but of the present and the future. God, in his grace, has forgiven us *all* our trespasses.

Contrary to what many people think, this knowledge sets us free, not to indulge in sin, but to be more responsive to God's demands of love, and to truly live in the Spirit. Jesus said, *"If the Son shall set you free, you shall be free indeed"* (John 8:36). We have not been set free so that we may indulge ourselves, but to live for him. Paul raised the question and then answered it in Romans 6:1, 2, *"Shall we go on sinning so that (God's) grace may increase? By no means!"*

Therefore, don't continue to indulge in the luxury of wallowing in your guilt. If you have been truly born of the Spirit, then begin to thank God for his forgiveness. Then ask him to give you the strength to live the kind of a life you know he wants you to live.

Meditate upon the following Scriptures that speak of God's gracious forgiveness.

Is. 1:18 *"Come now and let us reason together, says the Lord, Though your sins are as scarlet, they will be as white as snow; though they are red like crimson, they will be like wool."*

Is. 43:25 *"I, even I, am the one who wipes out your transgressions for my own sake; and I will not remember your sins."*

Is. 53:6 *"All of us like sheep have gone astray, each of us has turned to his own way; but the Lord has caused the iniquity of us all to fall on him."*

Ps. 32:1 *"How blessed is he whose transgression is forgiven, whose sin is covered!"*

Ps. 103:12 *"As far as the east is from the west, so far has he removed our transgressions from us."*

Rom. 5:8 *"God demonstrates his own love for us in this; while we were sinners, Christ died for us."*

Eph. 1:7 *"In him we have redemption through his blood, the forgiveness of sins, in accordance with the riches of God's grace."*

1 Pet. 2:24 *"He himself bore our sins in his body on the cross, so that we might die to sins and live for righteousness."*

1 John 1:9 *"If we confess our sins, he is faithful and just, and will forgive us our sins and purify us from all unrighteousness."*

FOLLOWERS
CHRISTIAN INDUCTION CENTER
DISCIPLES WATCH YOUR HEAD

FOUR
Disciple or Follower?

So, now that you have gotten the old guilt problem under control, how about becoming a disciple? "Wait a moment," you object, "I thought I became a disciple when I received Jesus as my Lord and Savior."

No, there is a big difference between being a follower of Jesus and being his disciple. He had followers by the hundreds, but comparatively few disciples.

The word *disciple* is used over 200 times in the Gospels, and in the very broadest sense it designated all the followers of Jesus. But Jesus himself gave it a very exclusive definition.

Listen carefully to his words in Luke 14:26–33: *"If anyone comes to me, and does not hate his father and mother, his wife and children, his brothers and sisters, yes, even his own life, he cannot be my disciple. And anyone who does not carry his cross and follow me cannot be my disci-*

ple. . . . And any of you who does not give up everything he has cannot be my disciple."

Here Jesus imposed three very stringent demands upon those who volunteered for discipleship. First, he said that a disciple must have love for Christ as his highest priority. We must love him even more than our family or dearest friends.

Of course, when Jesus spoke of hating our loved ones, he was speaking comparatively. He simply meant that we must love them less than we love him. As a matter of fact, this is how Matthew interprets Jesus' statement. He says, *"He who loves father or mother more than me is not worthy of me"* (Matt. 10:37). That is, our earthly affections are to be despised, compared to our devotion to the Lord. That's a tall order. But we have no right to call ourselves disciples if we are not prepared to make this our highest priority.

Second, according to Jesus, the one who aspires to be his disciple must be willing to lay his life on the line. This is what is meant by his reference to carrying our crosses. This implied more than a willingness to endure a few trials. We must understand it in the context of the day in which Jesus lived. At that time, to carry one's cross indicated that one was condemned to die. Therefore, Jesus was saying, *"Unless you are willing to lay down your life for my sake, you cannot be my disciple."*

Dietrich Bonhoeffer caught the deeper dimension of this when he said in his book *The Cost of*

Discipleship, "When Jesus calls a man, he bids him come and die."

So Jesus says, You cannot be my disciple unless you are willing to expose yourself to the risk of physical suffering, and possibly even death. That hundreds of thousands of believers over the course of centuries literally carried their crosses to the death for his cause, is a matter of historical record.

And then, just to reemphasize the quality of discipleship that he demands, he added, *"So therefore, any of you who does not give up everything he has, he cannot be my disciple."* What this means is, if we want to really become his disciples, we must raise our sights a little higher than Christians have been accustomed to raising them. It is more difficult than joining a church, or "slipping up one's hand while every head is bowed." It is total commitment.

If you really want to become his disciple, then you must be willing to say, "From this moment on, God helping me, Jesus Christ shall have supreme control over my life, my family, my future, my resources, my ambitions, and my destiny."

It is this kind of radical commitment that separates the Disciples from the Followers. Which do you want to be?

Matt. 7:13, 14 *"Enter through the narrow gate. For wide is the gate and broad is the road that leads to destruction, and many enter through it. But small is the gate and narrow the road that leads to life, and only a few find it."*

Matt. 7:21 *"Not everyone who says to me 'Lord, Lord,' will enter the kingdom of heaven, but only he who does the will of my Father who is in heaven."*

Matt. 16:24, 25 *"Jesus said to his disciples, 'If anyone would come after me, he must deny himself and take up his cross and follow me. For whoever wants to save his life will lose it, but whoever loses his life for me will find it."*

Phil. 1:29 *"For it has been granted to you on behalf of Christ not only to believe on him, but also to suffer for him."*

2 Tim. 2:3 *"Endure hardship with us like a good soldier of Christ Jesus."*

FIVE
Getting to Know You

In the book *Anna and the King of Siam* which was later made into a hit musical called *The King and I,* Anna sings about her experience as a missionary teacher in Siam, in getting to know the many children of the king of Siam. She sings, "Getting to know you, getting to know all about you, getting to like you, hoping that you like me too."

Now that you have begun your Christian journey, one of your priorities will be to get to know your sovereign Lord. It is interesting that God has already anticipated this need, and has provided a means whereby we can communicate with him. It is called *prayer*.

Immediately this brings to mind a flood of images. You might tend to harken back to your childhood and recall your first memorized prayer, "Now I lay me down to sleep." Or, it may conjure up in your mind the image of an ornately

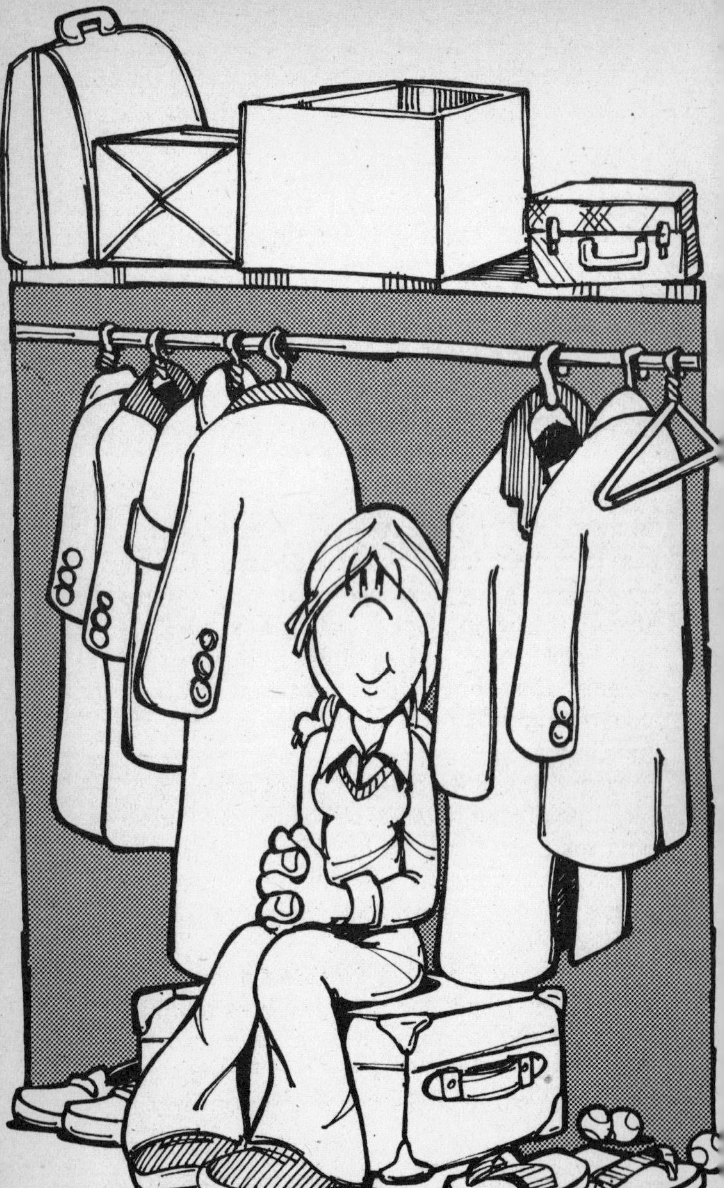

robed minister or priest standing behind a large pulpit and praying with ecclesiastical oratory. If you have come from a very religious family, you may call to mind the memory of a mother or dad kneeling with the children in the home and praying individually for each member of the household.

Prayer is probably one of the most difficult and misunderstood areas of the Christian life you will ever encounter. One would think that everyone would jump at the chance to talk with the Creator of the universe, and as often as possible. Oddly enough, this is not the case. People who have been followers of the Lord for many years have said that prayer was one of their most difficult disciplines. You can be very sure that our archenemy will do everything in his satanic power to prevent us from praying. Someone has well said,

*Satan trembles when he sees
The weakest saint upon his knees.*

Perhaps the best place to begin is by describing the different types of prayer. Most of us are familiar with the pastoral prayer, where the leader prays publicly on behalf of all of us. As the pastor "leads" in prayer, he anticipates our wishes and concerns, and articulates our desires. This form of public prayer is not wrong, but it is insufficient. What if the one leading in prayer fails to anticipate accurately my need? Perhaps he has no way of knowing what my real needs are.

Another form of prayer is that which is done in

small groups. Here, two or more people gather together and share their requests, then pray for each other. This is much more personal and specific. In small group praying, more than one person participates, and all pray together in *intercession* (on behalf, or for the cause of another). Every Christian needs a small circle of trusted prayer partners, who can join together in this very personal kind of praying. It might be well to look around for those who share your concerns, and to meet together for prayer.

But by far the most satisfying and rewarding prayer is the kind that Jesus recommended when he said, *"When you pray, go into your room, close the door and pray to your Father..."* (Matt. 6:6). You say, "That sounds like a great idea, Lord, but what do I say when I get alone with God?" You might begin by saying, "Hi, God, I'm in here." Then just talk to him about all those things in which you are interested and concerned. Don't be afraid of boring him, because he is intensely interested in you and your concerns.

Many Christians find it helpful to pray aloud when talking with God. Of course God can hear you whether you speak out loud or not, but sometimes it helps to articulate your thoughts. Furthermore, it tends to keep your mind from wandering. Also, be sure to allow some time for God to speak to you. It isn't courteous to monopolize a conversation.

Christians often ask which is the most important kind of prayer, the leader type, the group type, or the individual type. The answer is, we need all three for a well-rounded prayer life. We can profit immeasurably from the public prayers of God's servants. And we can be greatly helped by the more intimate prayers of a small group of concerned friends. But neither of these can be an adequate substitute for our private times of prayer, when we get alone with God.

I said at the beginning that prayer was a most mysterious subject. There are a number of philosophical problems involved with it. For one thing people often object, If God knows all about us, then why tell him about the needs of which he is already aware? But this argument expresses a very incomplete and inadequate concept of prayer. Prayer is more than a recitation of our needs and wants; it is an expression of our personalities, and an involvement of our beings. It is, in fact, an intimate fellowship with the Lord, which goes far beyond the realm of simple petition. My communication with my wife and children is not merely a recitation to them of my concerns, it is a sharing of my life with them.

Prayer is also an act of praise, whereby we extol the merits of God. We praise him, not only for who he is, but for what he has done.

Another objection has been raised concerning the plausibility of God hearing the prayers of his children all over the world at the same time. In our childish way we have pictured God sitting at a giant switchboard, frantically plugging and unplugging telephone connections. But all this betrays a very inadequate knowledge of the nature of God. J. B. Phillips expressed this dilemma in his book with the provocative title, *Your God Is Too Small*. Obviously, if we think of God in purely human terms, then this could be a problem. But we must remember that God is all-powerful, all-wise, and everywhere present. He said through Isaiah, *"My ways are not your ways, and my thoughts are not your thoughts."* Therefore it poses no problem for God to be in communication with his children at any time and any place. For our God *"neither slumbers nor sleeps."*

In spite of all the objections that have been raised concerning prayer, there is one unanswerable argument. Prayer works. It has been amply demonstrated through the ages that prayer has the power to change circumstances, attitudes, and situations. But even more than that, prayer changes *us!* The primary purpose of prayer is not to change circumstances, but to change us, to fit us to accept and adjust to circumstances that are under God's sovereign control.

Begin now to establish a regular and meaningful prayer life. Make this a top priority of your new Christian experience. For without it you are bound to be ineffective and unfruitful. The following Scriptures will be of help to you if you memorize and study them:

> John 14:13 *"Whatever you ask in my name, I will do it, that the Father may be glorified in the Son."*
> John 14:14 *"If you ask anything in my name, I will do it."*
> John 15:7 *"If you abide in me, and my words abide in you, ask whatever you will, and it shall be done for you."*

John 15:16 "You did not choose me, but I chose you and appointed you that you should go and bear fruit and that your fruit should abide; so that whatever you ask the Father in my name he may give it to you."

John 16:23 "Truly, truly, I say to you, if you ask anything of the Father, he will give it to you in my name."

John 16:24 "Hitherto you have asked nothing in my name; ask and you will receive, that your joy may be full."

1 John 3:22 "And whatever we ask we receive from him, because we keep his commandments, and do those things that are pleasing to him."

1 John 5:14 "And this is the confidence that we have in him, that if we ask anything according to his will, he hears us."

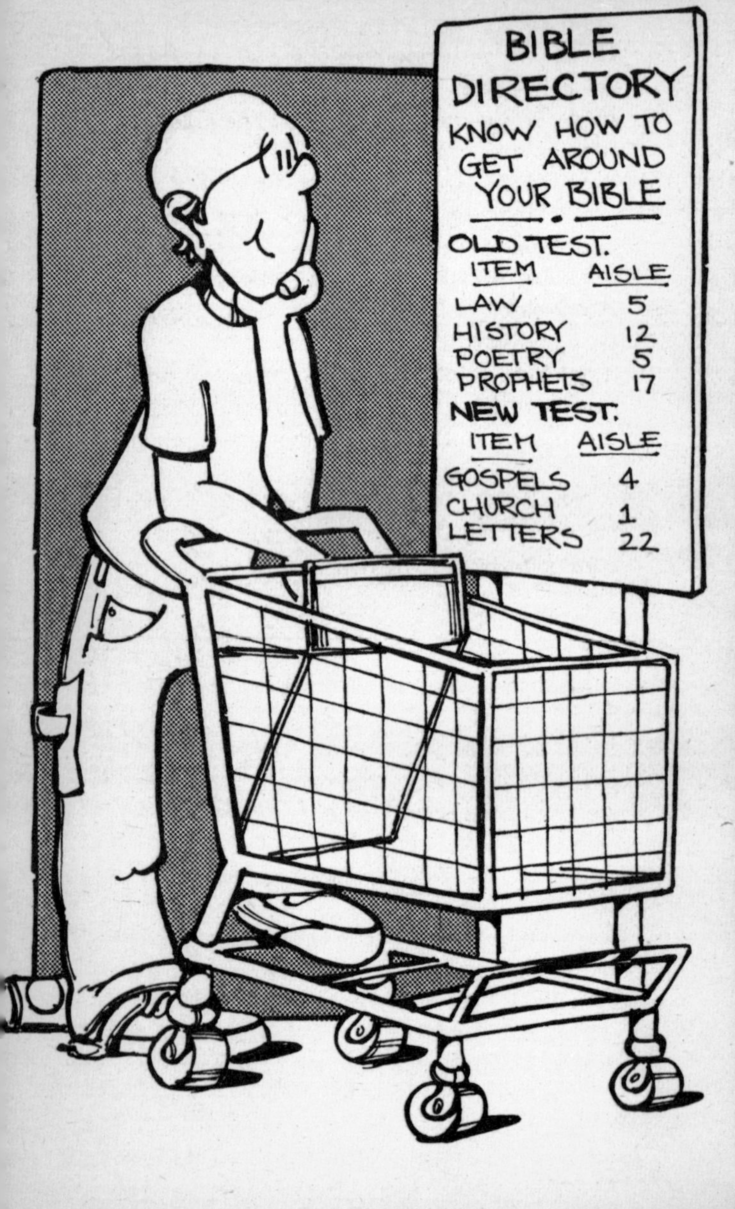
BIBLE
DIRECTORY
KNOW HOW TO
GET AROUND
YOUR BIBLE
OLD TEST.
ITEM AISLE
LAW 5
HISTORY 12
POETRY 5
PROPHETS 17
NEW TEST.
ITEM AISLE
GOSPELS 4
CHURCH 1
LETTERS 22

SIX
Getting Zonked with Begats

Having resolved to know the Lord a little better, you will want to begin to understand the Bible, for it is a revelation about God and his activities in the universe.

"That's a good idea," you say, "but I don't know where to begin. After all, the Bible is a pretty big book." I well remember my first encounter with the Scriptures. When I became a Christian, I picked up a copy of the Bible and did what came naturally. I opened it up to page one and started reading. In no time my head was spinning. I did well with the Adam and Eve account, but when I got to the fifth chapter I began to get mired in the genealogies of the patriarchs.

Then someone said, "Oh, you shouldn't start reading the Bible from the beginning. You should read the New Testament before plunging into the Old." That didn't make much sense to me, since I had been taught from kindergarten that it was correct procedure to begin reading a book from the beginning and not from the middle. Nevertheless, I dutifully turned to the first chapter of the New Testament and began again. Immediately I got zonked with "begats." *"Abraham begat Isaac, Isaac begat Jacob, Jacob begat Judah . . ."*

That was somewhat discouraging, but I treaded water until I got through that chapter. Then things began to get interesting. From chapter two until the end of the New Testament I could hardly put the book down.

So to save you the trouble of taking this circuitous route, let me make a few suggestions concerning your study of the Bible, give you a little information about how we got our Bible, and tell you about its structure. Don't panic, this will not be an involved exercise in academics. While the study of these things is a very intricate and technical science, we are not going to get bogged down in the mechanics.

WHERE DID THE BIBLE COME FROM?

Because the Bible is the primary source of our knowledge about God, man, origins, and destinies, it is well to know how we got it. Is it truly a miracle book, or is it, as many people say, merely a compilation of ancient myths?

I recall asking a junior high Sunday school class if anyone knew where the Bible came from. One girl replied timidly, "I think they found it in the bullrushes." That was about as good a guess as any, but it wasn't quite accurate.

It is important that we settle this question in our minds once and for all. For if the Bible is not miraculously inspired by God and miraculously preserved, then it is only another book and the product of mere human genius. When St. Paul wrote to the Thessalonian Christians, he commended them by saying, *"When you received the word of God which you heard from us, you accepted it not as the word of men, but as it actually is, the word of God..."* (1 Thess. 2:13).

We are faced with the question, Where did the Bible come from? Who wrote it? Obviously God didn't hand the Apostles a leather-bound copy of the Scriptures, complete with maps and concordance. So how did it come into existence?

We know that when Jesus and the Apostles came upon the scene, almost 2,000 years ago, there were already copies of ancient writings called "The Law and the Prophets." This was a reference to the first five books of the Old Testament, which were written by Moses, as well as the writings of later historians and prophets.

During the time of Israel's development the significant events of those years were recorded by Jewish leaders and the divinely ordained prophets of God. These men transcribed their messages and their writings became a part of the permanent record of human history. Eventually there were thirty-nine of these documents included among the writings that were called the Old Testament.

The question naturally arises, Who decided which of the writings should be included in this volume, and which should be discarded? You have no doubt heard the expression, the *canon* of Scripture. No, this was not an ancient weapon which was used to shoot the Philistines. The word *canon* is a Greek word meaning "reed," or "measuring rod." When used in connection with the Bible, it referred to those writings which measured up to the high standards set by the religious leaders, who were recognized for their godliness, integrity, and scholarship.

Jesus and the Apostles had access to those same Old Testament writings, much as we do today. In fact, on several occasions he gave his endorsement to them. In Luke 24:44 he referred to the words *"which were written in the Law of Moses, and in the Prophets, and in the Psalms concerning himself."* Obviously Jesus regarded the entire Old Testament as authentic, and he urged everyone to *"search the Scriptures, for they testify about me"* (John 5:39).

I always get a special thrill out of reading the Old Testament and knowing that Jesus also pored over those same Psalms, prophecies, and historical accounts. As a matter of fact, he based his teaching upon the great principles found in the Old Testament.

HISTORICAL FACT OR HYSTERICAL FICTION?

So much for the Old Testament. But what about that other part of the Bible called the New Testament? As far as we know, Jesus never wrote anything for posterity. However, much of what he did and taught and many of the events of his life were written by those who were familiar with his ministry.

Four men—Matthew, Mark, Luke, and John—wrote down those messages and events. Each wrote in his own particular style, but what they wrote was inspired by the Holy Spirit.

People have asked, "How could those men have remembered with any degree of accuracy what Jesus said and did?" Humanly speaking, this would have been impossible. But the disciples were aided in their task by God the Holy Spirit, in accordance with Christ's departing promise that *"the Counselor, the Holy Spirit, whom the Father will send in my name, will teach you all things, and remind you of everything I have said to you"* (John 14:26).

Later, as churches sprang up all over the known world, the need arose for a means of communicating with each other. Therefore the Apostles wrote letters (called *epistles*) to those churches and to some of the leaders of those churches, giving counsel, instruction, and encouragement. The majority of these letters were written by Paul, but others were written by John, James, Jude, and Peter. These letters were cherished and preserved, and passed from church to church. They were recognized by the church as having divine authority.

Again, just as with the Old Testament writings, these Gospels and epistles were subjected to extremely close scrutiny. Those that bore the identifying marks of authenticity were included in the canon of the New Testament. Ultimately, twenty-seven of these writings were chosen and became known as the New Testament. So today we have a book called the Bible (from *Biblia,* meaning "little books") comprising sixty-six books. These were written by about forty different authors over a period of 1,500 years; yet there is a remarkable continuity of thought and progression of ideas throughout this unique volume.

THE DIRECTORY
When my wife goes shopping in a new store, she always stops to look for the store directory. This tells her where she can find everything from gifts to garments. In a sense this is what we need to do in trying to find our way through the Scriptures. After studying the directory we will know where to find most everything. If you will take the time to memorize the following brief outline, you will never be at a loss to locate essential biblical information.

I. The Old Testament (total of 39 books)
   A. The Books of the Law (5)
      Genesis, Exodus, Leviticus, Numbers, and Deuteronomy
   B. The History of Israel (12)
      Joshua, Judges, Ruth, 1 & 2 Samuel, 1 & 2 Kings, 1 & 2 Chronicles, Ezra, Nehemiah, and Esther
   C. The Books of Poetry and Prose (5)
      (sometimes called "The Writings")
      Job, Psalms, Proverbs, Ecclesiastes, Song of Solomon

- D. The Books of the Prophets (17)
  Isaiah, Jeremiah, Lamentations, Ezekiel, Daniel, Hosea, Joel, Amos, Obadiah, Jonah, Micah, Nahum, Habakkuk, Zephaniah, Haggai, Zechariah, and Malachi
II. The New Testament (total of 27 books)
  - A. The Life of Jesus (4)
    Matthew, Mark, Luke, and John
  - B. The Beginnings of the Church (1)
    Acts of the Apostles
  - C. The Epistles (letters) of the Apostles (22)
    1. Paul (14)
       Romans, 1 & 2 Corinthians, Galatians, Ephesians, Philippians, Colossians, 1 & 2 Thessalonians, 1 & 2 Timothy, Titus, Philemon, Hebrews (Hebrews does not bear Paul's signature, but has his style and content.)
    2. James (1)
    3. Peter (2)
    4. John (4) (including Revelation)
    5. Jude (1)

With this outline firmly in mind you will be able to locate certain information immediately. For example, if you want to read about the events of Jesus' life or any of his teachings, you would turn to Matthew, Mark, Luke, or John. Should you want to locate the Ten Commandments, you would know that they were to be found somewhere within the first five books of the Bible, called the Law. This would narrow your search considerably.

It is often surprising to new Christians to discover that the Bible does have structure after all. It is more than a miscellaneous collection of religious facts. It has been written by men inspired by the Holy Spirit, brought together by others trained in the science of linguistics, and preserved by the people of God for all time. Jesus promised, *"Heaven and earth shall pass away, but my words shall never pass away."*

It is important that you take the time to memorize and meditate upon the following Scriptures which relate to the subject of the Bible.

> 1 Thess. 2:13 *"And we also thank God continually because, when you received the word of God, which you heard from us, you accepted it not as the word of men, but as it actually is, the word of God, which is at work in you who believe."*
>
> 2 Tim. 2:15 *"Do your best to present yourself to God as one approved, a workman who does not need to be ashamed and who correctly handles the word of truth."*
>
> 2 Tim. 3:16 *"All Scripture is God-breathed and is useful for teaching, rebuking, correcting and training in righteousness."*
>
> Heb. 4:12 *"The word of God is living and active. Sharper than any double-edged sword, it penetrates even to dividing soul and spirit, joints and marrow; it judges the thoughts and attitudes of the heart."*
>
> Luke 24:44 *"He said to them, 'This is what I told you while I was still with you: Everything must be fulfilled that is written about me in the*

Law of Moses, the Prophets and the Psalms.' "
2 Pet. 1:20, 21 *"Above all, you must understand that no prophecy of Scripture came about by the prophet's own interpretation. For prophecy never had its origin in the will of man, but men spoke from God as they were carried along by the Holy Spirit."*
Matt. 24:35 *"Heaven and earth will pass away, but my words will never pass away."*

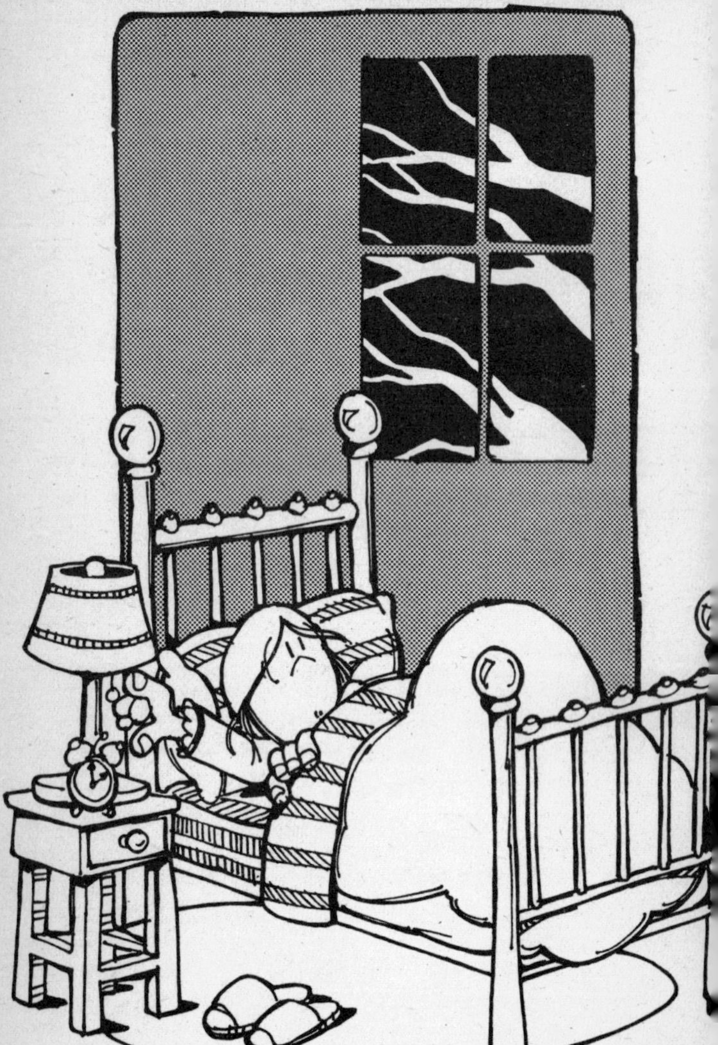

SEVEN
Is There Anybody Out There?

Did you ever lie awake at night staring into the darkness, and ask yourself, "Is there Anybody out there?" Somehow you instinctively knew that God was somewhere, but you sensed the need to be reassured. And did you ever ask yourself the question, "What is God like?" It is as normal as measles to think about these things.

A little girl expressed the frustration experienced by many in trying to learn something about God. She wrote,

I asked my mother what God was like,
    She did not know.
I asked my teacher what God was like,
    She did not know.
Then I asked my father, who knows more
    Than anyone else in the whole world
What God was like.
    He did not know.

*I think if I had lived as long as
My mother, or my teacher, or my father
I would know something about God!*

It is tragic that people can live a lifetime within the sphere of God's influence and yet know nothing about him. One great divine of several centuries ago said, "There is no greater subject that the mind of finite man can contemplate, than the subject of the infinite God." In this brief chapter we will discuss a few of the basic things we learn about God, as they are taught by nature, the Bible, human experience, and as they are revealed in Christ.

First, we learn that God is *spirit*. When Jesus talked with the woman at the well in John 4, he said, *"God is spirit."* That is, God is not flesh and blood as we are. When the Bible tells us that we are made in God's image, it refers to spiritual, not physical, qualities. It is true that the Bible speaks of God as having eyes, ears, hands, etc., but these are merely physical expressions to illustrate qualities of God's being. Since we see with our physical eyes, feel with our physical hands, and hear with our physical ears, it is very normal to think of God in physical terms. But God is spirit, and as such, he does not possess a physical body.

Furthermore, since God is spirit, he is invisible. John said in John 1:18, *"No man has ever seen God."* Paul speaks of the *"invisible God,"* one whom *"no man has ever seen,"* in Colossians 1:15, 1 Timothy 1:17, and 1 Timothy 6:16.

While it is true that God has revealed many

54

qualities and attributes about himself, it is also true that no living person has ever seen the full manifestation of God.

Second, God is *infinite*. The word *infinity* means "without bounds or limits." It is always hard for us with such limited minds to think in terms of the limitless. Have you ever stood on a hillside at night and looked out into space and wondered where it ended? There is no end to space—it is infinite. And so it is with God. No matter how far we can probe with the instruments of our technological age, we can not penetrate beyond the limits of the infinite God.

The Psalmist David must have experienced something of the wonder and awe of this when he wrote in Psalm 8:3, 4, *"When I look up into the night skies and see the work of your fingers—the moon and the stars you have made—I cannot understand how you can bother with mere puny man, to pay any attention to him!"* He also said, *"The heavens are telling the glory of God"* (Ps. 19:1).

God is infinite in duration. We often speak of human beings as being immortal. We are immortal in that once we are born we shall never cease to exist. The moment life is conceived in the womb it is destined for eternity. It might live for 100 years, or it might not survive birth, but it is immortal.

On the other hand, while we are immortal beings, we are not eternal in nature, for this implies no beginning as well as no ending. God is eternal in that he always existed and will continue to exist forever.

Furthermore, God is infinite in power. There is nothing that is beyond his power to perform. Jesus said, *"with God all things are possible"* (Matt. 19:26). And the Lord said to Abraham, *"Is anything too hard for God?"* (Gen. 18:14). Once this concept of an infinitely powerful God gets hold of us, it gives us a tremendous sense of confidence. For if God can create universes, and if he has control over all creation, then surely he can help us with our problems and needs.

Third, God is *personal.* He is not a mere abstraction or an impersonal force; he is a personal, loving heavenly Father.

The Mohammedans have ninety-nine names for God, but among them is not one "Our Father." It was our Lord and Savior Jesus Christ who taught us to address the God of the universe as *our* Father. That makes it extremely personal.

God is presented by our Savior as our heavenly parent, by John as a loving and kind God, by Paul as a God of justice and righteousness, and by the prophets as a God of judgment. All of these are qualities of personality found in some measure in all of us, but embodied in their fullness in a personal God.

But of all the qualities of personality found in God, none is so welcomed by us as the quality of love. We are overwhelmed by the thought that the God who presides over the vastness of the universe is deeply concerned about us. As the poet said,

*How Thou canst think so well of me
And be the God Thou art,*

*Is darkness to my intellect,
   But sunlight to my heart.*

Fourth, God is *everywhere*. The theologians call this *omnipresence*. David wrote, *"I can never be lost to your Spirit! I can never get away from my God! If I go up to heaven, you are there! If I go to the place of the dead, you are there. If I ride the morning winds to the farthest oceans, even there your hand will guide me, your strength will support me"* (Ps. 139:7–10).

A Sunday school teacher once asked her class of boys, "How many Gods are there?" A boy replied, "Only one." "How do you know that?" the teacher asked. "Cause there ain't room for no more," he said confidently.

How true this is. God fills the worlds with his presence. No matter where we go in this universe, even to the moon with the astronauts, God is there!

Yet, it is sadly true that people move about this little planet day after day with never a thought of God, oblivious to the fact that they are immersed in, and surrounded by him.

Helen Keller, before she was old enough to learn to talk, lost both her sight and hearing. For years she lived in a world of complete silence and total darkness. At nine years of age a dedicated teacher was hired, one who was a believing Christian. Through a process of painful and heartbreaking experiences, she was gradually able to penetrate that curtain of silence, and Helen began to learn.

The teacher felt that Helen should know

something about God, so she invited the famous preacher, Philips Brooks, to speak to her. When this godly man, through her teacher, told her about God and his love, to everyone's surprise this child said, "Oh yes, I have been hoping someone would tell me about him, I have been thinking about him for a very long time!"

Here was a child who, even though robbed of her sight and sound, instinctively knew that there was a God who loved her. And yet, many thousands of people without her handicaps are still woefully ignorant of God.

Aren't you glad that through Jesus you have come to know God as your heavenly Father? Yes, there is Somebody out there and we can know quite a bit about him.

Now, how would you like to try a little assignment? Take your Bible and begin reading through the Psalms. Write down everything you learn about God from David and the psalmists. You will be surprised at the length of your list. Better get a long sheet of paper.

EIGHT
A Crisis of Identity

Everybody keeps talking about an "identity crisis," and people are hung up on discovering who they are. For some reason this never bothered some of us, for we not only knew who we were, we even knew our own address and telephone number.

This is nothing new, for the people of Jesus' day faced a staggering problem of identity also. However, their problem was of a different nature. They had a great deal of difficulty in discovering who Jesus was.

This shows up in Matthew 16:13-16 where we read, *"When Jesus came to the region of Caesarea Philippi, he asked his disciples, 'Who do people say the Son of Man is?' They replied, 'Some say John the Baptist; others say Elijah; and still others say Jeremiah or one of the prophets.' 'But what about you?' he asked, 'Who*

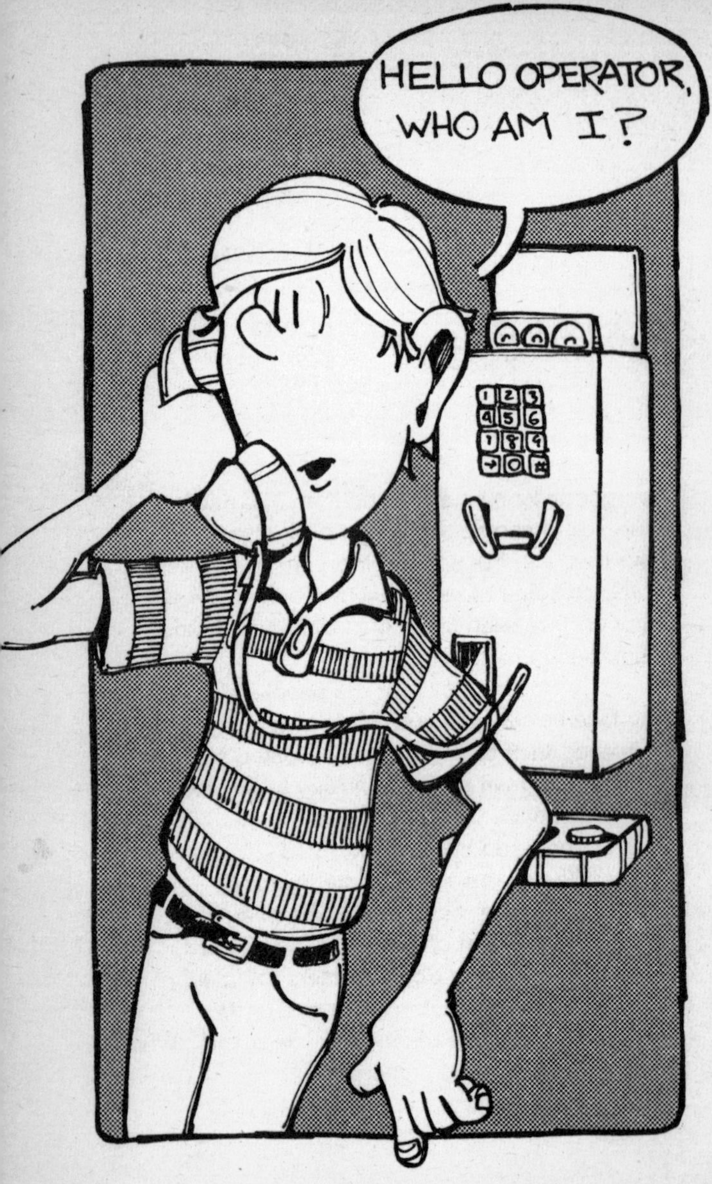
HELLO OPERATOR, WHO AM I?

do you say I am?' Simon Peter answered, 'You are the Christ, the Son of the living God.' "

Peter revealed some remarkable insight by his answer. He knew that Jesus was more than an Old Testament prophet resurrected, he was the living God's true and only begotten Son. This was a higher and grander concept of Jesus' true identity than that which his contemporaries held, or for that matter, than that which many people today believe to be true.

Our children used to sing a chorus, "Everybody Ought to Know Who Jesus Is." But the sad truth is that everybody doesn't know who Jesus is, including many pastors, theologians, church members, and Sunday school teachers. Like the people of the first century, many of these religious leaders believe Jesus to be just another great teacher. One noted writer said, "I am of the opinion that we can know next to nothing of the life and personality of Jesus, for the Christian sources (the Bible) are so fragmentary and so overgrown with legends."

Obviously many of our current theologians have an identity crisis. Fortunately for us, the followers of Jesus were not so confused. They went everywhere, covering their known world with the message of Jesus as Lord of the universe. *"And with great power the Apostles continued to testify to the resurrection of the Lord Jesus"* (Acts 4:33). They traversed the highways and the seaways telling everyone about Jesus, who he was, why he came, how he lived and died, how he was raised out of death and ascended to heaven, and how he would someday return to reign over all the earth.

Any attempt to cover the events of Jesus' life in a couple of pages is impossible. But I want to share a little outline with you that will help you summarize the information about Jesus. Then I would suggest that you read through the New Testament and that you fill in this outline with the verses you discover, putting them in their proper category. The outline is quite simple, and to make it even easier to memorize I have written it in alliterative form.

1. His Voluntary Incarnation

    The word *incarnate* simply means, "in the flesh." The Bible tells us that God, in the person of Jesus, came into our world in human form. He came "in the flesh," not as an angel or a spirit. *"And the Word (Jesus) became flesh and lived for awhile among us"* (John 1:14). In writing to his young protege Timothy, Paul said, *"The mystery of godliness is great: He (God) appeared in a body"* (1 Tim. 3:16).

    This is where the story of Jesus begins. It did not originate in Bethlehem. But ages before the worlds were formed, God determined to "incarnate" himself in human form, and to enter the stream of humanity. (We will see why he did this in a few moments.)

    So, contrary to what many people think, Jesus did not begin his existence in a tiny village of Palestine a mere 2,000 years ago.

But, as John the Apostle puts it, *"In the beginning was the Word, and the Word was with God, and the Word was God"* (John 1:1). As you trace the "Word" through the New Testament, you soon discover that it is a name given to Jesus. In John's last description of Jesus in Revelation 19:13, he wrote, *"He is dressed in a robe dipped in blood, and his name is the Word of God."*

But just as miraculous as his voluntary incarnation is the story of *how* God came into our world of time and space.

2. His Virgin Birth

God might have chosen to enter our world as a full-grown man with all the dynamic qualities of leadership that command universal acceptance. But to the amazement of the world, the angel pulls aside the curtain and reveals a tiny, helpless, dependent baby, lying in the arms of a human mother, and says, "Here is *God* manifested in the flesh!"

No wonder the world scoffed and said to the disciples, "You're putting us on! Do you expect the intellectual world of Greece and Rome to believe that tale?"

And yet, here is the story of Jesus and his birth, as told by the inspired witnesses. *"This is how the birth of Jesus Christ came about. His mother Mary was pledged to be married to Joseph, but before they began to live together, she was found to be with child through the Holy Spirit. Because Joseph her husband was a righteous man and did not want to expose her to public disgrace, he had in mind to divorce her quietly. But after he had considered this, an angel of the Lord appeared to him in a dream and said, 'Joseph son of David, do not be afraid to take Mary home as your wife, because what is conceived in her is from the Holy Spirit. She will give birth to a son, and you are to give him the name of Jesus, because he will save his people from their sins.' All this took place to fulfill what the Lord had said through the prophet"* (Matt. 1:18-22).

Here the Bible informs us that a young peasant girl from the remote village of Nazareth discovered that she was to have a baby. But this was not to be an ordinary child, for the Scriptures we have just noted inform us that this life was conceived in a supernatural way. The seed was not implanted in Mary's womb by man, but by the miraculous act of the Holy Spirit.

No wonder Mary's fiance, Joseph, found it impossible to believe! The story sounded so incredible to Joseph that he decided to break off his engagement, naturally thinking that Mary had been unfaithful to him and had made up this story. I imagine he stormed out of the house, saying to himself, "What kind of a fool does she take me to be?"

For this reason, the Lord made a special appearance to Joseph, to convince him that Mary was not lying. Mary's child had indeed been conceived by God, apart from any man. This is called by theologians the *Virgin Birth,* and it is a fulfillment of an Old Testament prophecy in Isaiah 7:14, *"A child shall be born to a virgin."*

Not only does the Bible speak about God's miraculous entrance into our world, but it goes on to describe his activity on earth.

3. His Virtuous Life

We are told that *"Jesus went throughout Galilee teaching in their synagogues, preaching the good news of the kingdom, and healing every disease and sickness among the people"* (Matt. 4:23).

Furthermore, the Scriptures stated that the Son of God lived a perfectly holy and sinless life. That is more than can be said of any of us. The men who lived with Jesus, and who ate, traveled, and slept with him, insisted that he was without fault or blame, and that he was without the stain of sin.

Peter, one who was very close to Jesus, said, *"Christ is our Lamb, without blemish or defect"* (1 Pet. 1:19). Paul referred to Christ as *"one who had no sin"* (2 Cor. 5:21). The writer of the Hebrew epistle said, *"he has been tempted in every way, just as we are, yet was without sin"* (Heb. 4:15).

So it is perfectly proper to refer to Christ's life as entirely virtuous. But there was good reason for this perfect life. For as God's remedy for man's sin and guilt, the Savior must be more righteous than the sinner. When the ancient Israelites symbolized the Savior's sacrifice for sins, they chose a perfect lamb from the flocks, one "without blemish or spot."

Therefore, Christ's virtuous life commended him to the world as the only true and perfect sacrifice for sins.

4. His Vicarious Death

The word *vicarious* simply means, "on behalf of another." So when we mention his vicarious death, we are defining the reason for it. Jesus died for us, on our behalf, in order to make full atonement for our sins. In a very real sense then, Jesus actually died our death, for we were condemned to death by our own sins. It wasn't for his own sins that he died, for as we have already seen, he had none. The law said, "the wages of sin is death." Therefore, as sinners, we were already condemned. But the good news of the gospel is, *"The wages of sin is death, but the gift of God is eternal life through Christ Jesus our Lord"* (Rom. 6:23).

In this passage we see death and life set in contrast. Death is the penalty for sin, but life is the reward of believing faith in Jesus. So when we say that Jesus gave his life vicariously, we mean that he actually died our death and paid our penalty, so that we might go free.

Here are just a few of the many references to this subject in the Scriptures. See how many others you can discover. *"He bore our sins in his body on the cross"* (1 Pet. 2:24). *"He was delivered over to death for our sins"* (Rom. 4:25). *"Christ died for the ungodly"* (Rom. 5:6). *"Christ died for our sins"* (1 Cor. 15:3). *"He gave himself for our sins"* (Gal. 1:4).

On the strength of all the scriptural evidence, it would seem incredible that anyone could miss this great truth. Yet, sadly enough, multitudes of people have failed to appropriate this simple fact that Jesus died for our sins.

5. His Victorious Resurrection

The story of Christ does not end at the tomb. All the Gospel writers insist that he was raised out of death by the power of God and that he returned to his original place in heaven. The biblical evidence for the resurrection is overwhelming. We have the authenticated records of the four Gospels, as well as the innumerable statements by the other Apostles. Furthermore, Luke says, *"After his suffering, he showed himself to these men and gave many convincing proofs that he was alive"* (Acts 1:3). Paul adds that Jesus was seen alive after his crucifixion by more than 500 eyewitnesses. (See 1 Cor. 15:4-8.)

It is conceivable that one or two witnesses might have been mistaken, but surely not 500! No court in the world could throw out that kind of evidence.

It was this certainty of his resurrection that enabled the early disciples to go out and proclaim fearlessly the message of the risen Lord. Had they doubted it for a moment they would not have been able to give up their own lives for this truth. Contrary to those who teach that the resurrection of Jesus was "spiritual" in nature, the Bible distinctly says he was "raised bodily."

6. His Visible Return

All of the New Testament writers were convinced that in the Lord's own time he would make his second appearance to our world. However, this time it will not be as a helpless baby in a manger, but as a strong, triumphant king! (We will discuss this further a little later.) But again, it is incredible that any serious reader of the New Testament could miss this great truth, for it appears more often than any other subject. Yet, surprising as it seems, the vast majority of professing Christendom is ignorant of it. Or, if they have read about his return, they do not think of it as a literal coming, but as a spiritual happening.

But one thing we can depend upon, our world is heading toward this climactic event with great rapidity. Sooner than we expect we will hear the great sound of the trumpet announcing his visible return.

As I requested at the beginning, I would urge you to memorize this simple outline of Jesus life; fill it in with the many other Scriptures that you discover as you read.

If Jesus were to ask you as he asked his disciples, "Who do you say I am?" could you give a satisfactory answer? I hope you can say as Thomas did, "My Lord and my God!"

NINE
Holy What?

Of all the subjects you will be discussing in the days to come, none will be so thoroughly confusing as that which deals with the Holy Spirit. The moment I picked up my first copy of the King James Authorized Version of the Bible and read about the Holy Ghost, I knew I was in trouble.

First of all, I had always been told that ghosts were not for real. Rather they were simply the inventions of adults for frightening little kids into being good. Then too, I had never heard of a ghost who was on the side of the good guys. They were always the heavies in the stories told around the campfire at night. Apparently they had only one purpose, and that was to scare the daylights out of people.

So with this background it isn't any wonder that new Christians are confused about a ghost who is for real and who is described as "holy."

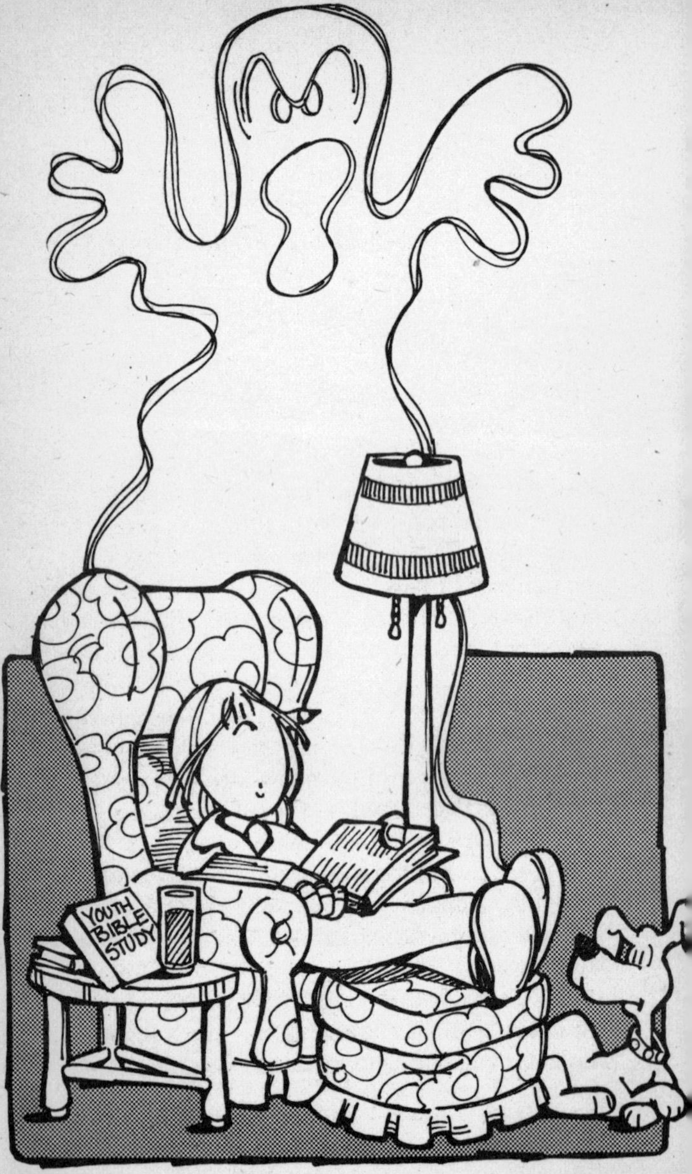
YOUTH BIBLE STUDY

All the later translations refer to the Holy *Spirit*. The Greek word *pneuma* doesn't help much, for it simply means "wind" or "breath." But the word *Spirit* seems to have a much better acceptance in our generation.

We must distinguish between matter and spirit. We ourselves are made up of both body (matter) and spirit. The body is the physical residence for our spirit. The physical part of us will eventually wear away and die. But that part of us which is spiritual in nature will continue to live forever. This is called *immortality*.

The Bible tells us that "God is spirit." That is, God has no physical body. Because he is spirit he is not confined to any one place, but is everywhere. This is called in theological language *omnipresence*.

When Jesus returned to heaven following his resurrection, he promised his disciples that he would send the Holy Spirit who would dwell within them and be their teacher, guide, and constant companion. He further promised them that when the Holy Spirit came to them, he would give them the ability to witness to everyone about Jesus. *"You will receive power when the Holy Spirit comes on you, and you will be my witnesses"* (Acts 1:8).

As you fellowship with Christians of varying church backgrounds, you will soon discover that there are differing opinions about the Holy Spirit and his ministry. The New Testament uses various expressions to describe the Spirit's activity. It speaks about being "baptized" with the Spirit, "filled" with the Spirit, and "empowered" by the

Spirit. Some Christians believe these are merely different ways of expressing the primary ministry of the Spirit to the Christian. Others teach that they represent different degrees of ministry to us. This is something you will want to study for yourself in more depth.

But for now it is important for you to know that the Holy Spirit does indeed dwell within you, and that he will strengthen you and enable you to live the kind of a life that is pleasing to God.

You might want to study and learn the following Scriptures that refer to these truths about the Spirit.

> John 14:16, 17 *"I will ask the Father, and he will give you another Counselor, the Spirit of truth, to be with you forever. The world cannot accept this Counselor, because it neither sees him nor knows him. But you know him, for he lives with you and will be in you."*
>
> John 15:26 *"When the Counselor comes, whom I will send to you from the Father, the Spirit of truth who goes out from the Father, he will testify about me."*
>
> Acts 1:5, 7, 8 *"'For John baptized with water, but in a few days you will be baptized with the Holy Spirit.' . . . He said to them: 'It is not for you to know the times or dates the Father has set by his own authority. But you will receive power when the Holy Spirit comes upon you; and you will be my witnesses in Jerusalem, and in all Judea and Samaria, and to the ends of the earth.'"*
>
> Acts 4:31 *"After they had prayed, the place*

where they were meeting was shaken. And they were all filled with the Holy Spirit and spoke the word of God boldly."

1 Cor. 12:13 *"For we were all baptized by one Spirit into one body—whether Jews or Greeks, slave or free—and we were all given the one Spirit to drink."*

IT'S NICE TO GET GIFTS

Everyone likes to get gifts, and Christians are no exception. Gifts tell us a great deal about the giver. They usually indicate love, generosity, understanding, and caring. The Bible talks about gifts given to us by the Holy Spirit. These have no reference to material gifts, but rather to abilities or talents given to us by the Holy Spirit to enable us to worship and serve God effectively.

Our first question is, What are these gifts? I have already indicated that they are God-given talents or abilities of various kinds. There are several places in the New Testament where Paul lists some of those gifts. It would be well to carefully read the following passages at this point, and then compile a list of them.

Rom. 12:4-8 *"Just as each of us has one body with many members, and these members do not all have the same function, so in Christ we who are many form one body, and each member belongs to all the others. We have different gifts, according to the grace given us. If a man's gift is prophesying, let him use it in proportion to his faith. If it is serving, let him serve; if it is teaching, let him teach; if it is encouraging, let him encourage; if it is contributing to the needs of others, let him give generously; if it is leadership, let him govern diligently; if it is showing mercy, let him do it cheerfully."*

1 Cor. 12:4–11 *"There are different kinds of spiritual gifts, but the same Spirit. There are different kinds of service, but the same Lord. There are different kinds of working, but the same God works all of them in all men. Now to each man the manifestation of the Spirit is given for the common good. To one there is given through the Spirit the ability to speak with wisdom, to another the ability to speak with knowledge by means of the same Spirit, to another faith by the same Spirit, to another gifts of healing by that one Spirit, to another miraculous powers, to another prophecy, to another the ability to distinguish between spirits, to another the ability to speak in different kinds of tongues, and to still another the interpretation of tongues. All these are the work of the one and the same Spirit, and he gives them to each man, just as he determines."*

Eph. 4:8–13 *"This is why it says, 'When he ascended on high, he led captives in his train and gave gifts to men.' (What does 'he ascended' mean except that he also descended to the lower, earthly regions? He who descended is the very one who ascended higher than all the heavens, in order to fill the whole universe.) It was he who gave some to be apostles, some to be prophets, some to be evangelists, and some to be pastors and teachers, to prepare God's people for works of service, so that the body of Christ may be built up until we all reach unity in the faith and in the knowledge of the Son of God and become mature, attaining the full measure of perfection found in Christ."*

Obviously Paul's listing was not intended to be exhaustive, but rather illustrative of the vast range of gifts available to the church. By comparing these passages, we can come up with a very accurate sample list of available gifts. There are different ways of outlining and arranging these gifts, but perhaps the following method will be helpful.

1. Gifts for spiritual leadership in the church
   Here Paul mentions the various areas of leadership: pastors, evangelists, prophets, teachers, and administrators.
2. Gifts for spiritual ministry to others
   These are the gifts needed to minister to the sick, the poor, and the discouraged.
3. Gifts for personal edification
   These are gifts of faith, tongues, interpretations, and spiritual discernment.

So we can see that the Holy Spirit has provided all the necessary resources for expressing the Word of God, both to the church and to the world.

The second big question is, Where do you and I fit into the picture? In other words, how do we receive these gifts? Obviously the Holy Spirit doesn't give all of these gifts to one person, but it seems evident that he does give at least one gift to each Christian.

It is also evident that we don't get these gifts of the Spirit by desiring them, pleading for them, or working for them. Paul says they are given arbitrarily by the Spirit to *"whomsoever he wills"* (1 Cor. 12:11). That is why they are called *gifts*. Gifts are given, not contracted for. Otherwise they are no longer gifts.

MISTAKES TO AVOID

There are two mistakes to avoid in considering the subject of the gifts of the Spirit. The first is the mistake of coveting the most spectacular gifts. Paul very explicitly warns against this. I have often wished that I had been gifted musically or with the power of oratory. And even more spectacularly, I have wished for the ability to heal people of any disease, and even raise the dead.

Obviously those gifts were not given to everybody. If they could be had by asking, every Christian in the world would possess them. It is also obvious that healing a person of terminal cancer is much more spectacular than taking a basket of fruit to a hungry family. But the same Spirit who gave the gift of healing also gave the gift of *"contributing to the needs of others"* (Rom. 12:8).

Therefore, do not be envious if the Spirit has gifted others with more exciting talents. Rather, begin to discover what your particular gift is, and then begin to develop it. For example, if you find that you have a God-given talent for giving encouragement, then begin to look around you for every opportunity to exercise this gift. Consider the possibility of visiting the sick, the aged, or the bereaved. Pray with them, read to them, minister to their physical needs. By so doing you will be exercising your gift, which the Holy Spirit has bestowed upon you.

A second mistake common among Christians is to expect that we must all receive similar gifts. Paul says *"there are different kinds of spiritual gifts"* (1 Cor. 12:4), and he shows how each member of the body has a distinct, though necessary, function. Therefore, it is unwise to expect or require other Christians to have received the same gift that God has given you. We must learn to leave the matter of the distribution of the gifts to the Holy Spirit, who alone can make this decision.

Let me encourage you to search out your gifts. You probably already are aware of these. These can sometimes be confirmed by asking your discerning Christian friends to honestly tell you what potential gifts they see in you.

Yes, it's nice to get gifts. But it isn't polite to indicate to the giver that you would rather have had something else.

THE FRUIT MARKET

Fruit that is rancid or rotten isn't worth much. I learned that lesson as a youngster when I went out to visit the farm. I recall seeing all kinds of apples lying around the foot of the trees, and wondering why more people weren't picking them up. After all, they were easier to gather than the ones in the trees. But upon biting into some of them, I discovered that they were overripe.

In the fifth chapter of Galatians Paul describes two contrasting kinds of fruit. The first is the fruit of the old sinful nature. In verses 19–21 he describes it as sexual immorality, impurity, debauchery, idolatry, witchcraft, hatred, jealousy, etc. This is rotten fruit; it is Paul's description of an ungodly, selfish, sensual life.

But in verses 22, 23 he speaks of *"the fruit of the Spirit."* These are qualities that describe the Christian who is living in the Spirit. That is, he is obedient to the moral, physical, and spiritual laws of God. What are those qualities? *"The fruit of the Spirit is love, joy, peace, patience, kindness, goodness, faithfulness, gentleness, and self-control."* For sake of convenience I have grouped them into three categories.

The first three speak of *inner qualities*—love, joy, and peace. In other words, the spiritual person is a loving, joyful, and peaceful person. You can't cut up each other, or speak in a spiteful way about your friends, or ridicule people, and show the fruits or evidences of being Christian. And you can't be effective in your witness for Christ if your life is as dismal and depressing as a soap opera. And you can't be a spiritual Christian if you are at war with yourself and others. These three qualities, love, joy, and peace, are evidences of the life of the indwelling Spirit.

The second group of three represent *conditions*

of relationship. Paul calls them *"patience, kindness, and goodness."* How do we handle the problem of the impatient spirit? We are much like the young Christian who prayed, "Lord, give me patience, and I want it right now!" It is so easy to become impatient in our relationships with others.

And what about the fruit of kindness? The truly spiritual Christian is one who exhibits the quality of kindness in his relationship with those around him. We all remember with shame some of the unkind things we have done to others, and the unkind and cutting remarks we have made. We need to show the gentle kindness of Christ in our interaction with others.

Then, closely allied with the quality of kindness is goodness. This is that innate goodness that sets a Christian apart from his peers. It was said of Jesus that *"he went about doing good."* We ought to occupy ourselves with the same mission.

The third group of three fruits mentioned involve *self-discipline: "faithfulness, gentleness, and self-control."* First, the spiritual Christian is a trustworthy person. He is the kind of a person who can be depended upon. When he promises to do anything, he always follows through. Second, he is a gentle person. He is not arrogant or cocky, nor overbearing and insolent. He does not belittle others, but he is gentle and loving in his contacts with others.

And last, Paul says that the spiritual Christian has self-control. (The word *temperance* means self-control.) The Christian who shows this fruit of the Spirit is able to control his temper, his appetites, and his passions. It is because the Spirit of

God is within him that he is able to bring these strong drives under control. It is self-control, but it is the self under the control of the Holy Spirit.

TEN
Dart Board Diplomacy

I'm sure every young Christian has felt like the guy in the cartoon in determining future decisions. How can we really know what God wants us to be, or to do?

A student once said to me, "I am totally frustrated and confused. I feel like I'm being pulled in a half dozen different directions. My father wants me to go into business with him, my pastor thinks I should go to seminary and prepare for the ministry, my friends all tell me I ought to be a lawyer, and my girl friend thinks we should get married this summer." Then he said, somewhat desperately, "What do *you* think?"

I replied, "It really isn't essential what your friends, pastor, parents, sweetheart, or even I think. You have only one issue to settle; namely, what does the Lord want you to do?" He looked at me a moment, then breathed a sigh and said, "Boy, that sure takes the pressure off!"

SCORING
1 2 3 4 5 6 7
POLITICS
FARMING
TRAVEL
MARRAGE
YOUR CHOICE

It is not uncommon for us to feel many pressures from different quarters when we are faced with large decisions. And it certainly is not wrong to seek advice of parents, friends, and other trusted people. But in the final analysis, the important consideration involves this thing we call "the will of God." There are no options about our course in life. As one great Christian once prayed, "The will of God, nothing more, nothing less, nothing else."

There are really three basic questions that every Christian must come to grips with here. The first of these is, Does God have a plan for my life? I am convinced that he does, and that the discovery of that plan is one of the most exciting adventures of life.

There are several valid reasons for this view. For one thing, our common sense should tell us that God never does anything aimlessly. There is purpose in everything he brings into existence. Take a look around you at the world of nature. Every part of God's creation has meaning. There is a perfect balance in nature that we have only recently begun to discover. That's what the ecological battle is all about. When Moses described the perfection of God's creative work, he summed it up by saying, *"And God saw everything that he had made, and behold, it was very good"* (Gen. 1:31). This indicates purpose.

But we don't need to be scientists to be aware of this. Just take a look at your own body. David said, "Thank you, Lord, for making me so wonderfully complex." I am sure that even David was not aware just how complex the human body and mind really is. It is awesomely intricate, and each part of it has a purpose to fulfill. So, it is logical to assume, based upon creation itself, that God has a purpose for every life that he has brought into being.

This is also verified by Scripture. Think of Jeremiah. God said to him, *"I knew you before you were formed within your mother's womb; before you were born I sanctified you and appointed you as my spokesman to the world."* Obviously God had a distinct plan in mind when he gave life to Jeremiah. This is also true of each of God's children; we are born for a purpose.

Therefore logic, Scripture, and personal experience answer the question, Does God have a plan for our lives? The answer is a resounding yes.

A second question is, What is the description of this plan? We are thinking now in general terms. Paul describes the will of God as *"good, pleasing, and perfect"* (Rom. 12:2).

First he says that God's will for us is "good." That is, it is not only intrinsically good, but it results in good. It is the same word he used in Romans 8:28 where he said, *"We know that in all things God works for the good of those who love him."*

This means then that even those things that appear to be working against us are actually working for us. There is the classic example of this in the Old Testament, where Joseph had been badly treated by his brothers, sold into slavery, and given up for dead. But Joseph prospered in Egypt, and eventually when he was reunited with his sheepish brothers, said, *"As far as I am concerned, God turned into good what you meant for evil"* (Gen. 50:20).

It may be that in the course of performing the will of God, we may face very difficult times. But be assured of this, *"God works for the good of those who love him."* So, the will of God for us is good.

Next Paul said it was "pleasing," or "acceptable." It is acceptable both to God and to us. You may be very sure that whatever God leads you to do or to be will not be distasteful. You will actually find pleasure in doing it, for God designs nothing for us without giving us the capacity to enjoy it. There are many Christians who will testify that at first they resisted God's will because they felt they would not enjoy doing what God had in mind. Then later, upon doing it, they found joy and fulfillment. The will of God is pleasing.

And Paul says it is also "perfect." That is, there is no flaw in it; it is ideally suited to us. Have you ever tried on a suit of clothes, or a dress, and had the salesperson say, "That garment was made for you, it fits you perfectly." That is what God says to us concerning his will.

This naturally leads to another very practical question: How can I discover the purpose for my life that is good, pleasing, and perfect? Will God write it upon the wall in flaming letters, will he shout it from the throne of heaven, or will he strike us down in the dust as he did Saul of Tarsus? The answer is probably none of these.

It appears to me that there are three primary

methods that God uses to communicate his will. One of these is in the *guidance of Scripture.* David described God's Word as *"a lamp unto his feet."* I do not know a truly alert and responsible Christian who does not rely heavily upon the Scriptures for guidance.

But there is also what the Bible calls the *witness of the Spirit.* This is that deep settled conviction that the Spirit gives as he assures us of our decision. When we make a right decision, it seems that the Holy Spirit gives us a deep settled sense of peace. And on the contrary, when we make a wrong decision, the Holy Spirit troubles us and gives us no real rest. I have found this to be a very reliable measure of the will of God.

Then of course, there is the matter of *human circumstance.* We must not forget that God is in control of the circumstances of our lives. And if the circumstances forbid our going in a certain direction, then, unless God changes those circumstances, we must conclude that this is not his will.

I remember a young man who felt called to the mission field, and asked my counsel. I pointed out to him several obstacles that were in his way. His wife was not a Christian, he had insufficient schooling, and their child was very sickly. Then I suggested that we pray about these barriers. We both prayed, but the circumstances remained unchanged. His wife did not come to Christ, his child was still quite ill, and he was unable to get training because of economic reasons. Today he is an active businessman serving God happily in his church and community. He is exactly where God wanted him to be.

No, we don't approach the subject of the will of God with a dartboard mentality. God is better organized than that. I am convinced that the Christian who sincerely wants to know the will of God, and who is willing to do it no matter what it is, will soon know. God doesn't enjoy playing games with us. He doesn't delight in keeping us dangling. *"Seek and you shall find."*

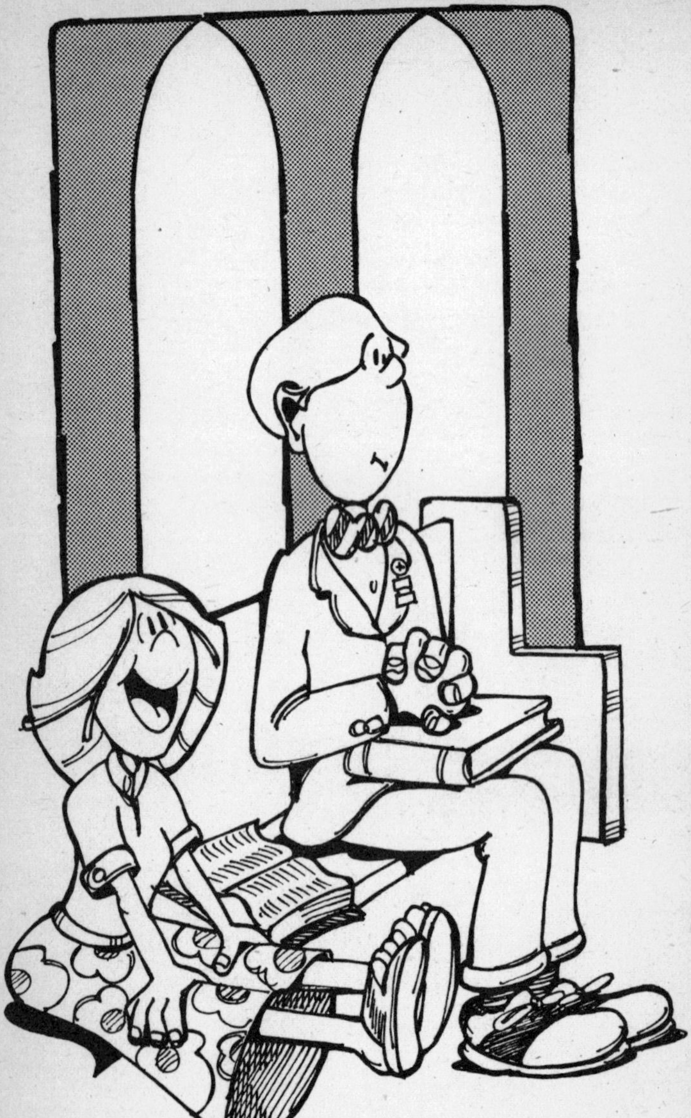

ELEVEN
Who Needs the Church?

One of the most amazing contradictions of modern times is the great variety of churches in the world. All claim to be patterned after the New Testament churches, yet they are so strikingly different. There are differences in style of buildings, form of worship, types of music, in the names and number of officers, in organizational structures, and even in habits and life-styles. One would think if churches today copied the New Testament churches there would be uniformity in these areas. The very fact that there is so much diversity would seem to indicate that the New Testament is not all that clear in these matters.

This in itself tells us something about God's design for the churches. Obviously he intended to allow a great deal of latitude in these areas, otherwise he would have been more precise. One of the reasons God has allowed differences in style of worship is because he has created us with differing temperaments and personalities. Some people who are quite structured and formal by nature will find themselves appreciating a style of worship that is more rigid and inflexible. Others who are much more informal and casual by nature will generally feel more at home in a church of that style.

Perhaps a brief word of background might be helpful to you in determining which church is for you. The word translated "church" is from the Greek word *ecclesia,* which means "called out." Originally the word applied to any persons separated into groups, such as citizens of a particular village or town. Later it came to have a more exclusive application to Christians, who were "called out" from the world to become God's people. In Matthew 16:18 Jesus spoke about "building my church." This had no reference to a physical building, but to a living body of believers. Each person who has received Jesus Christ as Lord and Savior is a part of his Church. You joined it, or rather, you were joined to it the very moment you became a Christian.

Originally the body of believers was very small, and the disciples received their fellowship and spiritual nourishment from Jesus himself. Following Christ's ascension it became necessary to meet together in local communities. Church groups sprang up in a number of cities in the Mediterranean area. These were called "local" churches, and while they were a part of the one body of Christ called the "Church," for convenience sake they met as local assemblies.

Today we are all familiar with the various

groups of churches called denominations. These consist of Baptists, Methodists, Lutherans, Catholics, and scores of others. These churches have banded together for various reasons. Some were drawn together because of similar doctrinal beliefs, some over methods of operation, and others over style of worship.

It has been argued that denominations are either a blessing or a curse. Some feel that the multiplicity of denominations provides a healthy option for the Christian, and that more can be accomplished as a denomination than as independent churches. Others feel just as strongly that denominations are divisive and present an image of disunity to the world.

Nonetheless, it is important that each Christian get involved in a local church. There are some good, sound reasons for this. For one thing, the church provides an excellent opportunity for united worship. While it is true that we worship God as individuals, we also need to worship as a group. We derive strength and inspiration from the united singing, praying, and praising by the body of believers. Thus as we corporately ascribe worth to God and lift our minds and hearts together in praise and adoration to him, we sense the unity of the body.

Affiliation with a local church also provides an opportunity for Christian fellowship. Here we meet others who know and love the Lord, and share a common bond. Barbra Streisand sings, "People who need people are the luckiest people in the world." If that is true, then we Christians are among the luckiest, for we need each other.

We are reminded in the Scriptures to exhort, encourage, and edify each other. We need this kind of reinforcement because we are engaged in spiritual warfare.

Another reason for involvement with a local church is that it provides an opportunity for the growth and development of our gifts for ministry. Within the body of Christ are spiritual leaders and teachers who can help us discover our gifts and talents, and more adequately equip us to serve the Lord. This is very important, for the church exists not primarily to serve us, but to provide us with an opportunity to serve.

There are other intelligent reasons for becoming involved with a church, but these which I have mentioned ought to be sufficient. We Christians do not exist in isolation. We are much like coals in a fire. Together we receive warmth from each other and we glow like the embers in the fireplace. But isolate a coal from the rest of the embers and it will soon die down.

There have been differing opinions through the years as to the function of the Church. Some think it exists primarily for evangelism, others believe its purpose is to train and nurture believers in the faith, and still others look upon the Church as a center of fellowship. Then there are Christians who are convinced that the central function of the Church is to minister to the needs of society and to be a healing agent in the midst of a hurting world.

Actually the Church of Christ ought to fulfill each of these functions. It should be involved in evangelism, teaching, fellowship, worship, and serving the physical and spiritual needs of the community. It should be a prophetic voice in the world, speaking out against injustice, oppression, and discrimination. It should be actively involved in promoting and supporting just social causes.

So, we come back to the original question, "Which church is for me?" This is a personal decision you must make after carefully evaluating the many churches in your community, and measuring them by these standards. Above all, don't keep floating from one church to another seeking to find the perfect church. There aren't any. Churches are made up of imperfect people, pastored by imperfect pastors. If you think you have found the perfect church, please don't join it, for then it would no longer be perfect.

Having said this, let me suggest some guidelines to follow in your search for a church.

1. Does it believe in the Bible as God's authoritative Word?
2. Does it have an outreach and ministry to its own community?
3. Is the style of worship practiced by the church consistent with your own God-given temperament?
4. Does it have a world vision that involves a ministry to the whole person?
5. Does it provide an opportunity for you to develop your gifts and talents for ministry to the church and community?
6. Are you in general agreement with the

doctrinal beliefs of the church? (You will never find perfect agreement in any church, unless you start your own.)

I hope you scored well on this exam. See you in church.

TWELVE
This Little Light of Mine

"Now that you have become a Christian, you must begin to witness." That's what everybody told me five minutes after I had made my decision to receive Christ as my Lord and Savior. But, for some strange reason, nobody told me what they meant by "witnessing." And I was quite surprised to learn that people had very different ideas about the subject. One older Christian told me that I wasn't really witnessing properly unless I was constantly giving out gospel tracts. She always kept her purse jammed with these pamphlets, and she never missed an opportunity to give them away.

An older Christian gentleman who was deeply involved in rescue mission work among the derelicts of society told me that I should be going down to the mission on Saturday nights and giving my "witness." The youth leader of our group was equally convinced that the most effective

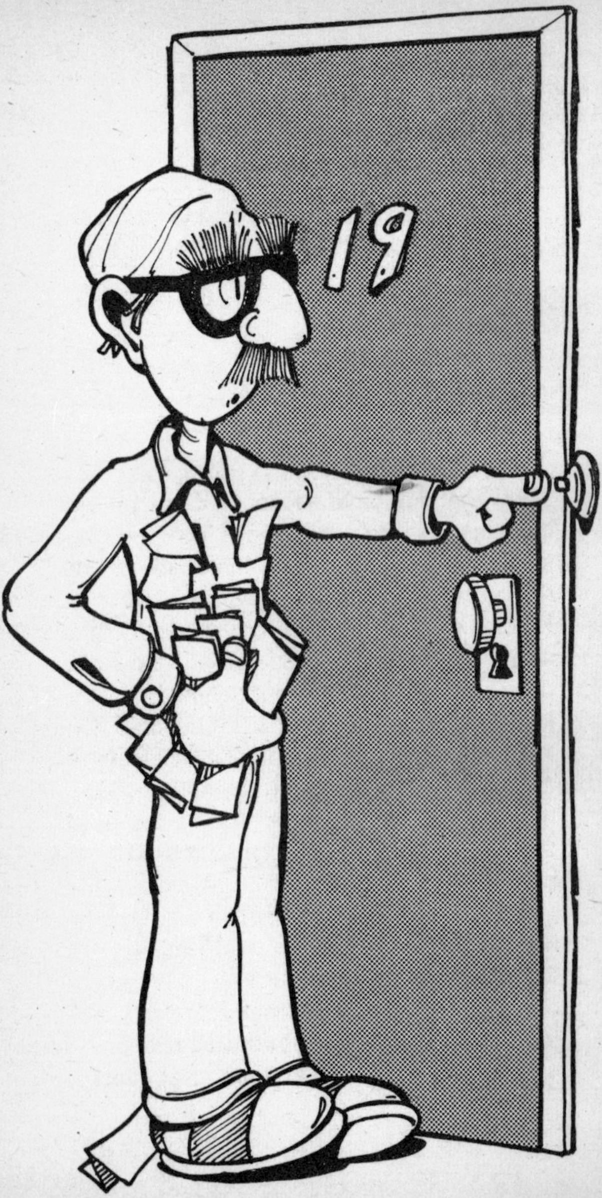
19

form of witnessing was down on the street corner, "just like Paul," singing and giving a public testimony. Others said that unless I prepared for a witness overseas in some foreign land, I would be settling for "second best." Consequently I gave considerable thought and prayer to becoming a foreign missionary.

In no time at all I found myself so tied up in street meetings, rescue mission witnessing, tract distribution, and church work that I became bogged down. Witnessing had become a burden and a bore. I was filled with all kinds of guilt about not getting "results." This meant, "getting souls saved." It became obvious to me that I was spending a lot of time spinning my wheels and getting nowhere.

So I will be forever grateful to a very mature pastor who took me aside and gently explained to me what witnessing was all about. He was right on target; so much so that after these many years of being a witness for Christ, his advice is still current. Let me share it with you.

Being a witness is much more important than witnessing. In our zeal to serve the Lord we often confuse the two. I know a man who spends hours preparing Sunday school lessons, giving out tracts to everyone he meets, and speaking at missions and clubs. He even includes a scriptural text on his business stationery. But sad to say, he is a very poor witness. Witnessing is more than *doing*, it is *being*. The man I referred to has no witness to his family or immediate neighborhood. The reason is simple. His life and conduct is not compatible with his message.

This is not intended to put down those who pass out tracts, give testimonies at rescue missions, and witness on street corners. These all have their place and have proved very effective in many instances. But none of these can be successful unless coupled with a consistent Christian life.

The other side of the coin is equally important. We must be prepared to give an oral witness whenever the Holy Spirit opens up the opportunity. The Apostle Peter said, "Always be prepared to give an answer to everyone who asks you to give the reason for the hope you have" (1 Pet. 3:15). The silent witness of a holy life is necessary, but so is the oral witness. Your neighbor might be impressed with your high moral lifestyle, but this doesn't explain to him that Christ died for his sins, nor does it explain the way of salvation. He could go to hell admiring your way of life!

So trying to witness for Christ without being a witness is like trying to row a boat with one oar. You will simply find yourself going in circles.

Another important fact to remember is that not all witnessing can be standardized. Our style of witness usually varies according to our temperament and personality, which are God-given. By nature some Christians are very gregarious, outgoing, jovial, and confident. They are the kind of people who can easily engage strangers in conversation. Other Christians might have been given a quiet, shy, contemplative kind of temperament. This is not a fault. Indeed, it is often a strength. One of the biggest mistakes we make in this matter of witnessing is to assume that these personality differences should merge, and that we should all witness in the same manner.

There are Christians who, by nature and temperament, can walk up to a total stranger at a bus stop and engage that person in conversation. That's great! But what about the Christian who is naturally shy? He is not at home among strangers in crowded rooms. Must he be squeezed into the same mold and be required to witness in a manner that is totally awkward to him? I do not think so.

It is my conviction that the Holy Spirit uses our differing personalities to witness in differing ways. I have met many young Christians who have been shamed into a style of witnessing that is unnatural to them and not consistent with their gifts. Such "forced" witnessing is not only unbecoming, but it makes the person to whom you are witnessing extremely uncomfortable, and it comes off as phony. God is not going to put you into a witnessing situation for which he has not equipped you.

Probably the best advice of all concerning witnessing was the last thing my pastor friend said to me. I had told him about all the books I had been reading about witnessing. I had read books telling how to witness to Jews, agnostics, Jehovah's Witnesses, and every other group imaginable. There were sample conversations to memorize, lead sentences to open with, arguments for every doctrine, and suggested answers for every conceivable question.

My pastor friend said in parting, "Go home,

clean out your book shelf, and throw away every book you have on how to witness. Then begin to live a godly, consistent Christian life at home, in your neighborhood and community." He added, "You will never need to force your witness on anyone. For when the Holy Spirit makes a person receptive to the gospel, he will give you the ability to share your faith with him."

That was the best advice I have ever been given concerning witnessing. And it still works.

Jesus said, "You are the light of the world. . . . Let your light shine . . ." (Matt. 5:14–16).

THIRTEEN
Where Do We Go from Here?

You can't read your Bible very long without becoming aware of a strong, insistent prophetic note. The writers of Scripture continually spoke of future times and seasons and referred to a return of Jesus to the earth again, cataclysmic judgments upon the earth, great satanic rebellions, the rise of Antichrist, a last great war, and a thousand-year reign of Messiah. These and a host of other events are predicted in the Bible.

For centuries Christian prophetic scholars have been trying to sort out all of these prophecies and place them in chronological order. They have also argued over the question of whether these events described by the prophets of the Old and New Testaments, and Jesus himself, were meant to be literal or figurative events. Most evangelical scholars have taken them literally.

I recall as a very young boy hearing about the possibility of the world coming to an end. I had

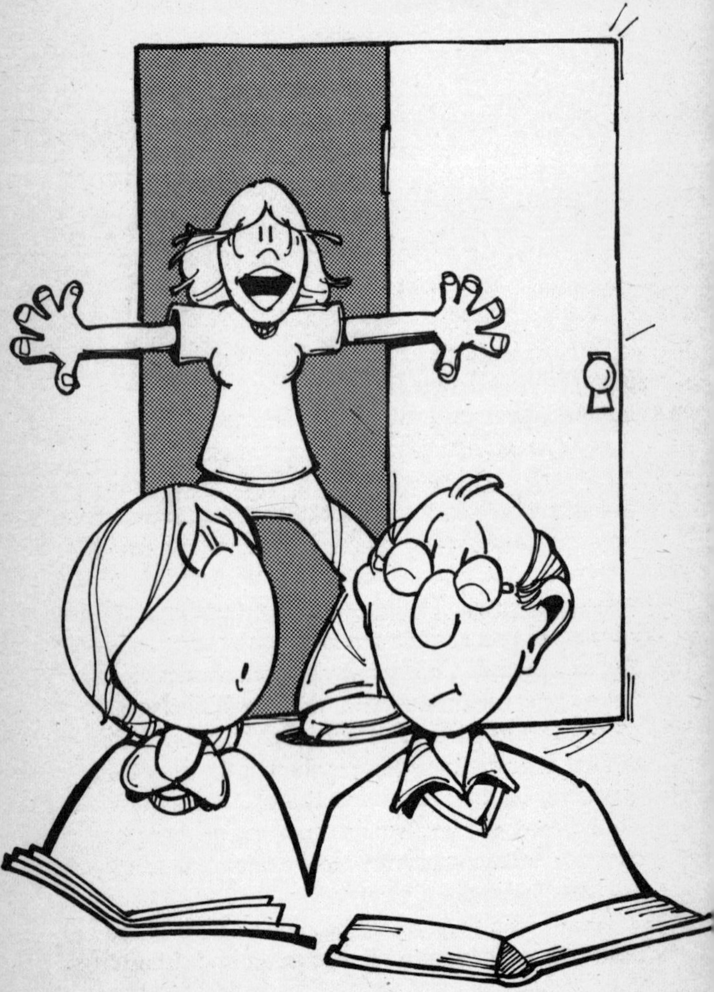

never been in Sunday school or church, so my information was second- or thirdhand. Nevertheless, I was so impressed by that knowledge that I lived in mortal fear for awhile. One summer evening I was sitting out on our front porch watching the sun go down. It was one of those summer evenings when the sun's reflection from the clouds turned the entire sky into a fiery furnace. I became very frightened and rushed into the house and made my first prophetic announcement, "The world is coming to an end!" For some strange reason my family wasn't greatly impressed.

Years later, after I had become a Christian and had begun reading the Bible for myself, I became quite interested in Bible prophecy. I remember attending a prophetic meeting held in a public hall where the lecturer had a huge chart strung up over the platform, extending from wall to wall. It was covered with strange, wild beasts, fire-breathing dragons, colorful horsemen, gold-colored thrones, and a brilliant, vivid lake of fire.

As he lectured he used a pointer to indicate various events as they are supposed to unfold. He had everything very neatly worked out in proper chronological order, and made it very clear that his was the only inspired outline of the future. Being very young in the faith and quite naive, I swallowed it all, hook, line, and sinker. And for years this chart formed the framework for my view of *eschatology* (last things).

After a few years of further study and maturity, I began to realize that I was having difficulty supporting my views from Scripture. Then I discovered that there were other views of these prophetic events and I have come to appreciate the prophetic Scriptures even more.

As I have indicated, most evangelical scholars believe the Bible teaches that there are certain events which are to happen in the future, although they do not all agree as to the chronology of these events. Therefore, the following list is not intended to be in any chronological order.

One of the events is that Jesus Christ is going to make a second appearance upon the earth in the future. This is called his *Second Coming*. And while he and the Apostles gave some hints as to certain indications or signs of his return, they all make it clear that no one will know the exact moment of his appearance. And yet in spite of this, you will find some preachers and authors making predictions about Christ's return and suggesting certain dates. Avoid them like poison.

Another event the prophetic Scriptures tell us about is a worldwide judgment, where the world will be judged for its sin and for its rejection of Jesus as God's provision for the sins of the world.

It also speaks about a "gathering" of believers at Christ's return. This is often called the *rapture* of the church. It simply means that all believers will be brought together to meet their returning Lord, and will be with him forevermore.

There is mention also of a period of unprecedented trial that is to come upon the people of the earth, called the *Great Tribulation*. Jesus said it would be extremely severe and would be of such drastic proportions that no one in history had ever seen its equal. The evangelical church has been divided in its opinion about the Great Tribulation period as it relates to Christ's return. For many centuries the church held that Jesus would return immediately after this period of trial (Matt. 24:29-31). Later some Bible students suggested that he would come back just prior to that Tribulation, and others have maintained that it would be in the middle of the Tribulation. There are good and godly scholars among the proponents of each of these views.

Just as there has been a difference of opinion about the Tribulation, as it relates to Christ's return, there has also been a dispute about the period of time called the *Millennium* (a thousand years). Some Bible scholars believe that Jesus will return before this Millennial reign, some believe his return will occur at the close of the Millennium, and still others are of the opinion that the Millennium is a figurative term and should not be taken literally.

The very fact that sincere and able scholars differ on the details of Bible prophecy would indicate that they are not all that certain. Therefore, it is always a good principle to observe that wherever there are these differences in details one should not be too dogmatic about his opinions. It is certainly not wrong to formulate your own ideas about these things, but it is unwise to insist that your own ideas are infallible. Beware of the prophetic teacher who will tolerate no other opinions but his own.

So, where do we go from here? When we die or when the Lord returns, what then? On this the Bible has some very positive answers. First, we know that we are going to be with Jesus. "I go to prepare a place for you. And if I go to prepare a place for you, I will come back and take you to be with me that you also may be where I am" (John 14:2, 3).

This tells us explicitly that the Lord has a place prepared for us. The Bible refers to this as *heaven*. It also informs us that Jesus is personally going to escort us to that place. Not only is he preparing a place for us, but at his return he will prepare us for that place. The Bible says, "Our citizenship is in heaven. And we eagerly await a Savior from there, the Lord Jesus Christ, who, by the power that enables him to bring everything under his control, will transform our lowly bodies so that they will be like his glorious body" (Phil. 3:20, 21).

In Paul's masterful discourse on this subject in 1 Corinthians 15 he describes this transforming event in some detail. (Read especially from verse 35 through the end of the chapter.) Here he says, "we shall all be changed." In other words, this perishable body will be instantly changed into a body like that which Jesus had at his resurrection—an imperishable body. That body will never decay or deteriorate, but will be immortal.

We are not told a great deal about this heavenly home we are to inhabit for eternity, but it will be indescribably beautiful. And because sin will not be present there, we will never have to experience the sad results of sin: death, disease, sickness, disappointment, or heartache. "And God himself will be with them and be their God. He will wipe every tear from their eyes. There will be no more death or mourning, or crying or pain, for the old order of things has passed away" (Rev. 21:3, 4).

Much more could be said about this, but it is sufficient for now to say that God has made every provision for his children to live with him forever. What a glorious and wonderful experience that will be. No wonder Paul said, "I desire to depart (this life) and to be with Christ, which is better by far" (Phil. 1:23).

As a new believer in Christ your eternal destiny is assured. The Lord Jesus Christ, who died to save you, will complete the job. He said, "I will never leave you, nor forsake you." That is more than a promise for this life—it is a promise for the life to come.

So, my young Christian friend, let us rejoice! We have a great future ahead of us. And while men are despairing of life all around us, we have a hope that goes beyond this temporal life. If we don't meet each other here, I'll see you in the hereafter. Happy journey!

Here is just a sample of the scores of verses that deal with the subject of last things. You ought to memorize these and keep adding to them as you continue to read the Scriptures.

Jesus' Second Coming
Matt. 16:27 *"For the Son of Man is going to come in his Father's glory with his angels, and then he will reward each person according to what he has done."*
John 14:3 *"I will come back and take you to*

be with me that you may also be where I am."
Acts 1:11 *"This same Jesus, who has been taken from you into heaven, will come back in the same way you have seen him go into heaven."*

Final Judgment (Read Rev. 20:11-15)
Acts 17:31 *"For he has set a day when he will judge the world with justice by the man he has appointed. He has given proof of this to all men by raising him from the dead."*
2 Tim. 4:1 *"Christ Jesus, who will judge the living and the dead . . . at his appearing."*

The Great Tribulation
Matt. 24:21 *". . . there will be great distress [tribulation], unequaled from the beginning of the world until now, and never equaled again."*

The Millennium (Read Rev. 20:1-6)

FOURTEEN
Keeping the Battery Charged

In concluding this series of subjects, perhaps we should come back to the place where we started. We began by talking about you and your new life of faith. If you are going to continue with Christ, then you will need more than biblical doctrine. There must be a daily application of that knowledge to your own personal devotional life.

Perhaps you have had the experience of attempting to start your car one morning, only to find that it is capable of emitting just a meager groan. You keep turning the ignition key harder, somehow thinking that this will help, but the motor still stubbornly refuses to turn over. "Dead battery!" you say, and you kick yourself for your failure to keep the water in the battery at the prescribed levels. You never intended to let this happen, but it was such a little thing, and so easy to forget.

Our devotional lives are much like that. We

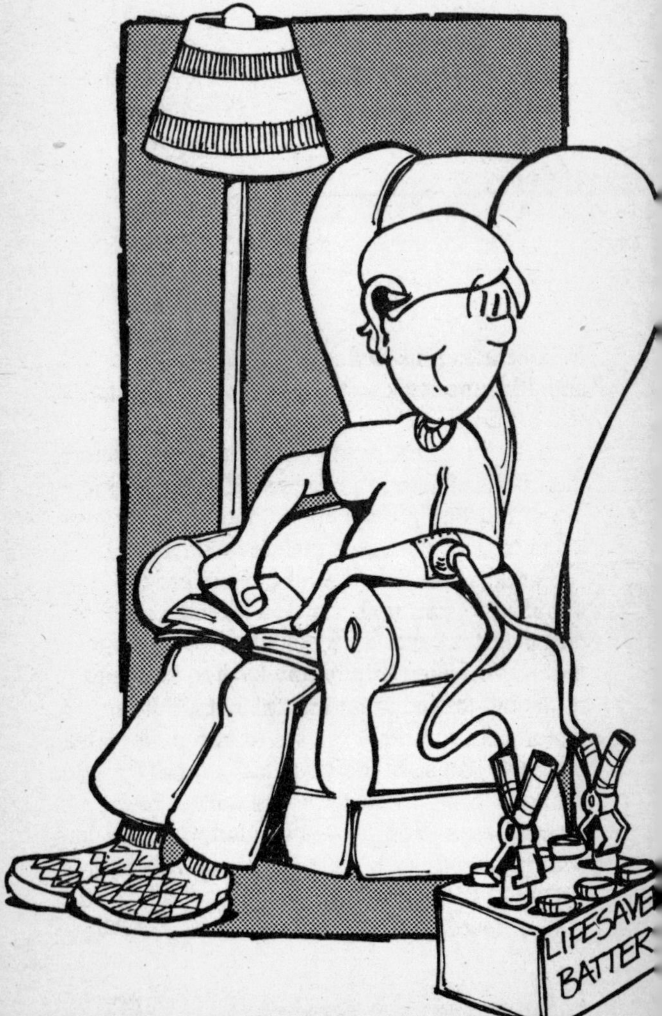
LIFESAVE
BATTER

remember to take care of the big things, but forget how important it is to keep the spiritual battery charged up. The best way to solve the battery problem is to regularly and systematically give it the attention it needs. If you are sincere about maintaining a strong devotional life, it will require the same kind of regular attention.

I do not know of any substitute for a daily devotional time with the Lord. I have been observing the Christian scene as a believer and as a minister for forty years and I have yet to meet a productive Christian who has not maintained a regular, systematic devotional life. Sooner or later his battery will run down and he will have to get a push to get the motor started.

"Okay," you say, "I'm convinced. How do I get started?" Here are some practical suggestions for establishing a devotional life:

1. Decide on the hour of the day best suited to you. This will depend on your daily activities. Some find it more convenient to set aside a time before breakfast, and some prefer bedtime. I know students who have their devotions at lunchtime. There really is no time that is more sacred than another. "God neither slumbers nor sleeps," the Bible tells us, so he will be ready when you are. For me, the bedtime hour was always a disaster. I am not a night person, and I found myself reading and praying without meaning. My spirit was willing, but my flesh was weak. However, I know many Christians who find the bedtime hour

the most meaningful. Then, it is usually quiet, the phone is not ringing off the hook, and it is an opportunity to reflect upon the day.

So, don't let anyone else set the time for you. Choose that time of day which fits your personal schedule and which you find to be the most beneficial.

2. Then, try to find an appropriate place. You may be one of those rare persons who can concentrate with the TV on, the radio blaring, the kids screaming, the dog barking, or the vacuum cleaner whining. But I think there is wisdom in Jesus' suggestion that we find a quiet "closet," and shut the door. That will take some doing if you are in a college dorm or have a number of brothers or sisters. But the old proverb, "Where there is a will, there is a way," is still valid.

3. Next, decide on the amount of time you can devote to this spiritual exercise. Again, it will vary according to your schedule. It is easy to get a guilt complex about this, especially when we read of the old divines who used to be up at five AM and spend three hours in prayer before breakfast. What they fail to tell you is that they not only got up with the birds, they went to bed with them also. I think most people try to average between twenty and thirty minutes of quiet time. You may be able to spend more time than that, but you can hardly afford less.

4. Having settled these logistical problems, the next question is, Now what? And it is at this point that most quiet times succeed or fail. Is

this to be a time of Bible study? Should it include a daily reading from a devotional booklet? Or should we spend the entire time in silent meditation and prayer?

Again, there is no biblical rule about how we spend this time with the Lord. It would have been nice if Paul had laid it all out in a neat little outline. Probably the reason he didn't is because we are at different levels of spiritual growth and we all have differing needs. Furthermore, we do not all express our worship of the Lord in the same way. I know a student who loves to take an old hymnbook with him and drive out to the park. He sings his way through the hymnal, meditating over every verse. For me, with my voice that would be a disaster.

Here I can only share my own personal preferences. I refer to this quiet time as a "devotional" time. It is not a time of in-depth Bible study, but a time for expressing my love and praise of the Lord. There are times when I begin by reading out loud from the Psalms. I do this from various modern translations. I spend part of the time in prayer. It has always been my custom to pray out loud because this helps me to express my thoughts. Perhaps like you, I am a great "wool gatherer," and if I try to pray in my mind, I soon find my mind wandering. Therefore I have found that I need the discipline of the verbalized prayer.

For variety, I have used devotional booklets, using the given Scripture before the reading of each day's thoughts. Usually these booklets are quite brief, and many are also quite light.

Some Christians prefer to use the quiet time for the study of Scripture. Again, this depends largely upon the individual preference. I prefer to study the Scriptures at another time, and to reserve the quiet time for a devotional reading of the Word. Since there are no inspired directions given for this in the Bible, the Lord must want us to have some latitude in the matter. Above all, be flexible. And if you want to avoid the problem of your quiet time degenerating into meaninglessness, use variety.

5. Finally, stick to it. You will find every reason under the sun for either postponing your devotions or discontinuing them. For sure, the Enemy will throw before us every stumbling block he can, and it will require all the discipline and spiritual stamina you can muster to climb over them. But don't forget, John said that "The one who is in you is greater than the one who is in the world," (1 John 4:4). So, if you have determined to begin a life of daily devotions, the Holy Spirit will help you overcome the hindrances of the "one who is in the world."

Have an enjoyable trip, but keep that battery charged up. While on the road, you might want to think and meditate over the following verses.

Psalm 5:3 *"Each morning I will look to you in heaven, and lay my requests before you, praying earnestly."*

Psalm 92:1, 2 *"It is good to say, 'Thank you,' to the Lord . . . every morning tell him, 'Thank you for your kindness,' and every evening rejoice in all his faithfulness."*

Psalm 119:9 *"How can a young man stay pure? By reading your Word and following its rules."*

Psalm 119:11 *"I have thought much about your words, and stored them in my heart so that they would hold me back from sin."*

Mark 1:35 *"Very early in the morning while it was still dark, Jesus got up, left the house, and went off to a solitary place, where he prayed."*

Matthew 6:6 *"When you pray, go into your room, close the door and pray to your Father, who is unseen."*

Mark 6:46 *"After leaving them [his disciples] Jesus went into the hills to pray."*

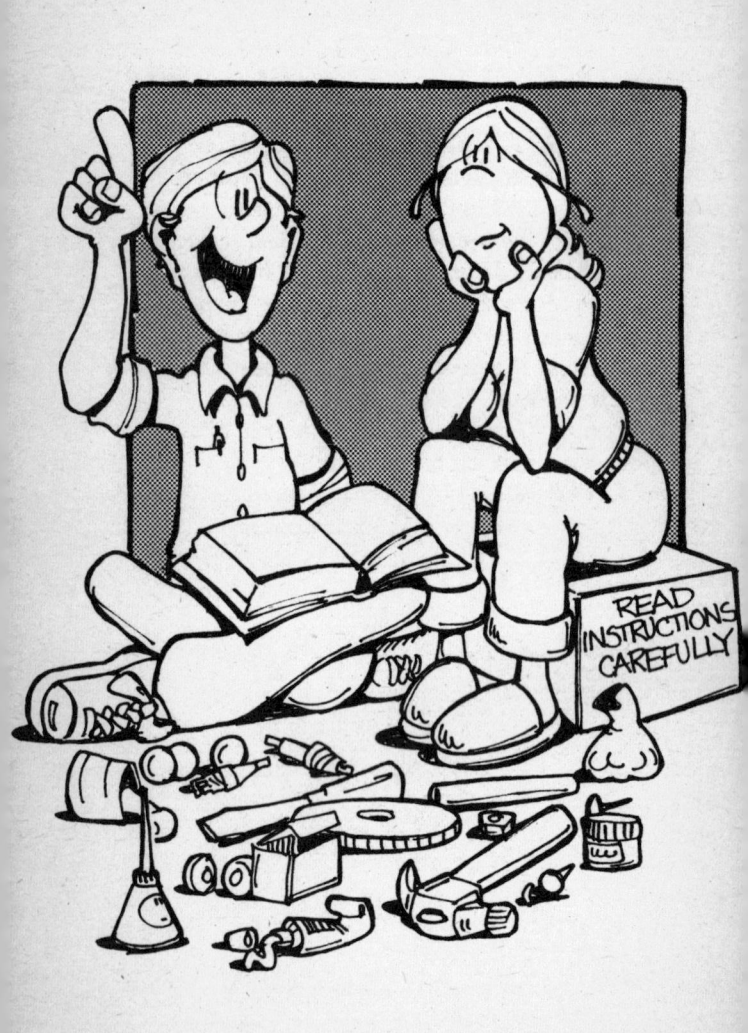
READ INSTRUCTIONS CAREFULLY

APPENDIX:
Recommended Books

While preparing a list of books as recommended reading I've gotten caught on a snag. Some books may be quite helpful to me, but be of no value to you. Some new Christians appreciate books written from the perspective of philosophy, others don't care to wade through the vocabulary of thought and ultimate meaning. Some Christians devour anything *apologetic* (that is, anything that proves or defends Christianity), but others who haven't got a mind for logic prefer something more personal. But of these people, some like devotional books while others are fascinated by the writings of the mystics and martyrs and saints. So it goes. I think you see what I mean.

Still, it seems important, so let me tread where angels fear to (and probably with good reason). I recommend most anything published by InterVarsity Press. They specialize in books, pamphlets, and Bible studies for young, sharp Christian men and women. I can likewise recommend Navigators' study guides, *Design for Discipleship,* and Campus Crusade for Christ materials. Campus Life literature is also very good.

But before you invest your money in expensive books, I suggest that you consult an evangelical pastor. A perusal of his personal library might help you weed out those books that would be useless for you and give you ideas about the titles you'd like to purchase. If your church has a library you should also make use of that. Then, when you go to a bookstore, one that specializes in evangelical materials, take your time. Browse through some of the books. Check the Tables of Contents. Believe me, caution here will save you time and cash.

The fourteen areas I have touched on in this booklet I hope will whet your appetite for more. You can find scores of books dealing with each of these subjects.

Perhaps right now you are beginning to empathize with the puzzled young man in the cartoon. There are so many pieces to put together. But remember, when all else fails, read the manual—the Bible.